GPvTS Fund

The Need for Certainty

International Library of Sociology

Founded by Karl Mannheim

Editor: John Rex, University of
 Aston in Birmingham

Arbor Scientiae
Arbor Vitae

A catalogue of books available in the **International Library of Sociology**
and other series of Social Science books published by Routledge &
Kegan Paul will be found at the end of this volume.

The Need for Certainty

A sociological study of conventional religion

Robert Towler

Routledge & Kegan Paul
London, Boston, Melbourne and Henley

To
Richard and Kim

Au 2230,
Hm 262 / GP
14/4/85

First published in 1984
by Routledge & Kegan Paul plc

14 Leicester Square, London WC2H 7PH, England

9 Park Street, Boston, Mass. 02108, USA

464 St Kilda Road, Melbourne,
Victoria 3004, Australia and

Broadway House, Newtown Road,
Henley-on-Thames, Oxon RG9 1EN, England

Set in 10/11pt Times
by Columns of Reading
and printed in Great Britain
by The Thetford Press Ltd., Thetford, Norfolk

Library of Congress Cataloging in Publication Data

Towler, Robert.

The need for certainty.
(International library of sociology)
Includes index.
1. Sociology, Christian. 2. Christianity – 20th century.
3. Religion. 4. Robinson, John A. T. (John Arthur Thomas),
1919– . Honest to God. I. Title. II Series.
BT738.T69 1984   306'.6   84-6810

British Library CIP data also available

ISBN 0-7100-9973-8

Contents

	Preface	vi
1	Varieties of religion	1
2	Exemplarism	19
3	Conversionism	38
4	Theism	55
5	Gnosticism	68
6	Traditionalism	80
7	Implications and conclusions	94
	Notes	110
	Appendix	120
	Index	127

Preface

For all that it is so slight, this volume represents the work of several years. The most arduous labour, the content analysis, was undertaken by Ross McLeod, Joyce Williams and Ruth Norris in 1973-5, and to them I am deeply indebted. The work was made possible by a grant from the Social Science Research Council, and by the generous support of the Department of Sociology at the University of Leeds, who put a research assistant at the disposal of the project for an entire year as well as allowing me to take a year's study leave, and I would like to record my gratitude, both to the SSRC and to the Sociology Department at Leeds.

Amongst the many friends and colleagues who gave their encouragement, particular thanks are due to John Robinson, who entrusted the original letters to me and became a respected friend. His death in December 1983 was a personal loss to many people, and I am privileged to count myself among the number. The letters are safe and bound for Lambeth Palace Library, which is just another tribute to his thoughtfulness, as his death approached, for coming generations of scholars. Thanks are due also to Zygmunt Bauman, whose characteristic wisdom transformed an interesting project into an exciting one, and to Hugh Bishop, whose own correspondence provided the original idea and whose combative support made it possible to write and re-write the book. Richard Toon and Steve Molloy contributed more than they knew by their enthusiasm at the end.

The author and publishers are grateful to Faber & Faber and to Harcourt Brace Jovanovich for their permission to reproduce the lines from T.S. Eliot's 'Burnt Norton' on p. 41.

1 Varieties of religion

My aim in this book is to describe some contrasting ways in which people can be religious. To state the aim in those terms immediately suggests a study of the great world religions, but in fact I shall be describing the variety which occurs within a single religious tradition, and at one point in time. So specific is the focus, indeed, that people representing these various ways of being religious might be at the same church service together, singing the same hymns, saying Amen to the same prayers, and listening to the same sermon. Because of the nature of the data on which the study was based the service these people attended would probably be one held in an Anglican church in England, but with minor variations these forms of religiousness almost certainly occur in Churches other than the Church of England, and in the rest of Europe and in the USA as well as in Great Britain.

So this is a study of very conventional religion in the latter part of the twentieth century. It is not concerned with the exotic, the remote, or the rare.

The point of conducting the study reported here, and of delineating different ways of being religious, is to make a contribution to the sociology of religion. I hope that what follows may be of general interest, but my principal intention is to promote better empirical investigations of contemporary religion by sociologists and we must therefore begin with a brief review of current perspectives in the sociology of religion in order to see why this study was necessary and how it fits into the contemporary debate.

The contemporary debate

The earliest work in the sociology of religion, from Comte and Spencer to Durkheim and Weber, was concerned with religion in relation to other social institutions. Some studies took religion as the dependent variable and sought to show how it was influenced by other social factors, while other studies took it as an independent variable and explored its effects on aspects of society as diverse as the economy and the suicide rate. Most of this work was based on historical and ethnographic data, and it was assumed that, whatever its role, religion was a social institution of major importance. Those early sociologists also commented on the religion of their own day, but on this subject there was not the same unanimity and there were broadly two opinions. One saw religion as the indispensable basis of any and every society, and in so far as they recognized the waning strength of Christianity the proponents of this view either sought to discern emergent functional alternatives or, after the fashion of Saint-Simon and Comte, promoted alternatives of their own inventing. The other opinion took Christianity to be manifestly in decline and, on the grounds that western civilization was the most advanced form of society to have emerged, inferred that religion everywhere would be progressively eroded. This opinion too assumed two forms, for while Marx regarded the demise of religion as an indication of social maturity (as Freud was to regard it as a sign of personal maturity), Weber took a more equivocal view and saw the spread of rationality as a social advance but also as a belittling of the human spirit.

Now these two opposing interpretations are of more than historical interest for they stand at the head of two contrasting perspectives in the sociology of religion. Both are still very much alive, and one, following Durkheim,[1] has continued to look for beliefs, experiences and practices which have on them the stamp of the sacred. Work in this tradition has been descriptive and analytical, while research which has been informed by the other perspective, which has thought of itself as more Weberian,[2] has tended to be quantitative, and has attempted to plot the decline of religious institutions empirically.

The most influential single monograph in the Durkheimian tradition was undoubtedly Thomas Luckmann's *The Invisible Religion*,[3] but we can now see that it marked both a beginning and an end for the work which employs that perspective. It marked a beginning in that Luckmann abandoned the search for a set of ideas which are treated as sacred by all the members of a society. Durkheim had recognized that any such ideas had, in his own time, yet come to be 'formulated', but more than forty years later Luckmann, recognizing that nothing had emerged, proposed a more radical solution. Durkheim had believed that 'so long as there are human societies, they will provide from within themselves great ideals for men to serve'.[4] Luckmann, by contrast, was willing to see a new form of religion rather than a religion which would succeed Christianity: 'What are usually taken as symptoms of the decline of Christianity may be symptoms of a more revolutionary change: the replacement of the institutional specialization of religion by a new social form of religion.'[5] He suggested an altogether more voluntaristic model than Durkheim could have contemplated, in which there is a 'sacred cosmos', but one which no longer 'represents *one* obligatory hierarchy' and which 'is not articulated as a consistent thematic whole'. He spelled out his model thus:

> It may sound like an exaggerated metaphor if one speaks of the sacred cosmos of modern industrial societies as *assortments* of 'ultimate' meanings. The term points out accurately, however, a significant difference between the modern sacred cosmos and the sacred cosmos of a traditional social order. The latter contains well-articulated themes which form a universe of 'ultimate' significance that is reasonably consistent in terms of its own logic. The former also contains themes that may be legitimately defined as religious; they are capable of being internalized by potential consumers as meanings of 'ultimate' significance. These themes, however, do not form a coherent universe. The assortment of religious representations – a sacred *cosmos* in a loose sense of the term only – is not internalized by any potential consumer as a whole. The 'autonomous' consumer selects, instead, certain religious themes from the available assortment and builds them into a somewhat precarious private system of 'ultimate' significance. Individual religiosity is thus no longer a replica or an approximation of an 'official' model.[6]

Since Luckmann's monograph was published an increasing number of sociologists of religion have begun to study the assortment of religious themes from which people make their choice, and to study the choices made. In this respect Luckmann's work represents a beginning.[7]

In two other respects *The Invisible Religion* marked the end of an era. In the first place it was the last major contribution to the sociology of religion to use the word 'religion' to denote beliefs and ideas with no super-empirical or supernatural reference, as Durkheim had done. Because the word is used to refer to such a bewildering array of things we must rapidly review the current usages.

1 Conventional religion. Alternatively called official religion and church religion, conventional religion includes the principal religions of the world and their long-established sub-divisions. It should be noted that the size of a group does not detract from the conventional character of a religion, as we see in the case of ethnic minorities.

2 Sectarian religion. The religion of the sects is distinguishable from that of churches and denominations not because the beliefs are different, but because sects have 'a totalitarian rather than a segmental hold over their members'.[8]

3 New religious movements. The plethora of first-generation organizations fall under one heading only very uneasily, but they share three characteristics. Firstly, because they are movements in their first generation, they do not provide a 'tradition' for devotees to join or appropriate. Secondly, although commitment to these groups can be intense, it has an experimental quality, not least because of the youthfulness of the first generation, and indeed some groups do not expect more than a partial and provisional commitment.[9] Thirdly, the beliefs and practices are not unambigiously religious, often focussing on techniques and knowledge which claims to be more than 'merely religious' *vis-à-vis* conventional religion.

4 Popular religion. This category, too, is diffuse, and as well as being called popular religion[10] it is known as folk religion,[11] common religion,[12] and 'subterranean theology'.[13] It includes the religious beliefs, practices and experiences which are traditional and pervasive in a society, and yet which lie outside the prescriptions of conventional religion, often, indeed, being discouraged or proscribed by dominant religious institutions of the 'great tradition'.

5 Civil religion. This term, from Rousseau, has been employed by Robert Bellah in describing the modern USA: 'there actually exists alongside of and rather clearly differentiated from the churches an elaborate and well institutionalized civil religion.'[14]

6 Surrogate religion. In the older Durkheimian tradition there are those who have continued to identify such things as communism, psychoanalysis and humanism as surrogate religions,[15] or to see science fiction, rock climbing, or the arts as forms of implicit religion.[16]

7 Invisible religion. Coined by Luckmann, this term has gained wide currency in the meaning described above. For more than

twenty years there has been a move to restrict the word 'religion' to beliefs and practices with a supernatural referent,[17] and since the appearance of *The Invisible Religion* it has become common practice to do so. Luckmann recognized that, even under the changed conditions, conventional religious institutions 'continue to be *one* of the sources contributing to the thematic assortment of the modern sacred cosmos',[18] but subsequent authors have adopted a different terminology. If 'religion', as beliefs and practices relative to supernatural things, is but one species in a larger genus, what should we call the genus? Luckmann was content to retain the word religion, but later writers have not.

His work marked the end of an era in a second respect because sociologists who have explored the genus within which religion has a place have tended to conduct empirical and quantitative studies. Luckmann was the last sociologist of note to pursue the Durkheimian perspective at an abstract level, for the tradition has now been affected by the empiricism which formerly characterized the tradition of those who saw themselves as following Weber. How, then, has the genus been described?

Robert Wuthnow has examined what he calls 'meaning systems'.[19] In using the term 'meaning system' he does not intend to identify the pattern of beliefs held by an individual or a group of individuals, but a set of symbols, material and non-material, which has an independent existence. Thus Calvinism, as Weber described it, would constitute a meaning system. Wuthnow identified four meaning systems, and then conducted a survey in the San Francisco Bay Area in 1973 in order to 'identify people who found each of these symbol systems meaningful and to compare these people in order to examine the behavioural and attitudinal orientations associated with each symbol system'.[20] This stage of his work was strictly empirical. The meaning systems themselves, however, were not empirically derived, but identified as ones which have 'enjoyed prominence in American culture'.[21] The four he identified were:

1 Theism: God is the agent who governs life.
2 Individualism: The individual is in charge of his own life.
3 Social science: Life is governed chiefly by social forces.
4 Mysticism: The meaning of life and the forces that govern life cannot be understood by the human intellect.

Each meaning system, as will be clear, is thought to supply 'a distinct understanding of the meaning and purpose of life'.[22] Although the meaning systems studied by Wuthnow are interesting, their value is severely limited by the fact that they are not empirically derived. His study could therefore confirm their salience to a greater or lesser degree, but it could not test their existence, and still less identify others.

Rodney Stark and William Sims Bainbridge, who are embarked upon an ambitious project to construct a 'general theory of religion',[23] have criticized Wuthnow and suggested that only Theism, the religious option, is a 'true' meaning system. They conducted their own study to 'explore the distribution of the meaning systems in a social network and examine mutual influences, mediated by interpersonal relationships, between the meaning systems and social experimentation',[24] because of their conviction that 'meaning systems exist only as they have *social* meaning'.[25] In their view, only empirically established constellations of attitudes which can be shown to be associated with social networks should count as meaning systems. Thus in Luckmann's terms they would be uninterested in the 'assortment' of themes available, and prepared to study only those themes which have been chosen. They are similarly unimpressed by Wuthnow's meaning systems as objectively existing sets of symbols, and are prepared to countenance only world-views in which they can be shown to occur, rooted in social relations. This criticism of Wuthnow by Stark and Bainbridge is damaging only because he is unable to produce independent evidence for the existence of the meaning systems whose implications he studies. Stark and Bainbridge themselves are wedded to two unfashionable views: that only conventionally religious beliefs articulated by social organizations are worth sociological attention,[26] and that secularization is simply not occurring.[27] Their empirical findings in support of the latter view will be awaited by many sociologists. The former view does not admit of empirical support, and such evidence as exists is open to other interpretations, as is true of the findings of Stark and Bainbridge in their test of Wuthnow's thesis.[28]

William McCready and Andrew Greeley illustrate the recent trends clearly. They are chary of using the term 'religion':

> We would prefer to talk about the 'sociology of basic beliefs' or a 'sociology of ultimate values' because we are convinced that 'religion' is not limited to dogma, doctrine, devotion, or ritual, but rather is a set of cultural convictions concerning the individual's, or the society's, perception of a transcendent reality. These convictions may become manifest in a body of doctrine, or in ritualistic practices, or even in ecclesiastical structures over a period of time, but it is not a corollary of

their existence that they will.[29]

Like Wuthnow, they were working in the early 1970s, and anxious to proceed empirically. Like Wuthnow, they were not clear about which meaning systems or systems of ultimate values they should investigate, but at least they were clear that they were not clear:

> Having decided to attempt to measure basic meaning systems, we were faced with the problem of what the likely sets of interpretations might be in American society. Since no one had approached this question before, there was no literature to fall back on for guidance. What was the possible range of responses to ultimate issues available to humankind in contemporary America – or, indeed, to humankind at any time in its history? We finally decided to take our cue from Paul Ricoeur's classic mixture of anthropology, archaeology, comparative religion, and philosophy, *The Symbolism of Evil*.[30]

Following this cue they decided upon six 'interpretative responses' to 'ultimate questions of good and evil':

1 Religious optimism: 'God will take care of everything, so there is no need to worry.'
2 Secular optimism: 'Everything will turn out for the best somehow.'
3 Grateful acceptance: 'We must be grateful for the good things that have happened to us despite the bad things that we have to endure.'
4 Anger: 'It is unfair and unjust that we should have to suffer.'
5 Resignation: 'There is nothing that can be done; what will be will be.'
6 Hopefulness: 'There is no denying the evil of what is happening, but the last word has not been said yet.'[31]

Prompted by a suggestion from Clifford Geertz, they employed an imaginative technique with respondents, describing six imaginary situations and asking which of a list of reactions respondents might have. The first of these items, for example, was:

> You have just visited your doctor and he has told you that you have less than a year to live. He has also told you that your disease is incurable. Which of the following statements comes closest to expressing your reaction?[32]

A final example of this kind of work is a research programme at Berkeley reported by Charles Glock and Thomas Piazza. Like McCready and Greeley, they are conscious of the absence of a literature to guide empirical investigations, but they took their lead from Peter Berger and Thomas Luckmann and looked for what they call 'reality structures'.[33] As their starting point they took the question: 'How do people deal with experiences and events which call for a judgement about how the world works?' But again, like McCready and Greeley, and like Wuthnow, they were anxious to begin empirical work. The approach they describe recognizes the possibility that preliminary empirical studies need to be undertaken, but like their colleagues they proceeded on the assumption that they did know at least something, and that more would be discovered in the process of undertaking research. So they write:

> The assumptions people hold about the structure of reality, we considered an empirical question, to be answered by the type of research we began to envision. It required no new research, however, to specify at least some of the assumptions we would encounter. Philosophers, theologians, scientists, and pseudo-scientists have been speculating for centuries about forces which influence human events and shape social life. From among these forces we chose the following as probably among those to which ordinary citizens might refer when trying to account for events which happen to them or to which they are exposed. . . .[34]

They asked, 'To what extent do you believe your life is influenced by . . .' and their list was as follows:

1 Environment: 'The way you were brought up.'
2 Luck: 'Luck.'
3 Supernatural: 'God or some other supernatural force.'
4 Conspiratorial: 'What people in power decide.'
5 Individual: 'Your own will power.'

This third example closely parallels the work of Wuthnow and of McCready and Greeley, and the objections raised by Stark and Bainbridge might have been levelled against any of the three pieces of work.

I raised a problem in respect of Wuthnow's work and that problem deserves to be restated here, for it applies to this approach in general. The meaning systems which these scholars have investigated were all identified *a priori*, and this gives rise to two difficulties. In the first place we cannot know whether they exist as meaning systems, or whether the clusters of attitudes which are found to be associated with them in empirical studies have a significance of their own while in no way flowing from the *a priori* meaning systems. This difficulty would be resolvable by statistical techniques, at least to a degree, were it not for the second difficulty. Having once identified a set of meaning systems, subsequent research sets about the task of examining their correlates. By its very nature, this procedure must tend to confirm the existence of the categories with which it starts since it is designed to explore their consequences, not to test for their presence. Assuming that the meaning systems are identified as provisional categories only, the best one can hope for is that some will be dropped when they are selected by too few respondents. Even this is hazardous, however, for the researcher will be tempted to think that a faulty operational definition and set of items is responsible for the lack of responses, and will be more inclined to reformulate the questionnaire than to drop the meaning system. Worst, however, is the fact that this research design precludes the discovery of unanticipated meaning systems: they exist *a priori* or not at all. This is an intolerable weakness for it presumes that social scientists are omniscient and rules out the possibility of finding what one did not know was there. In practice, of course, research does not proceed on a unilinear path, and one hopes that the numerous informal feedback loops might obviate some of the difficulties just identified. But in theory this research design is sadly deficient.

One further and final problem is indicated in the opening sentences of the critique of Wuthnow by Bainbridge and Stark. These doughty opponents write that:

A powerful tradition among sociologists of religion is to regard human beings as theologians and philosophers. It assumes that people almost universally possess a relatively coherent, overarching, and articulated 'Weltanschauung', 'world-view', 'perspective', 'frame of reference', 'value orientation', or 'meaning system'.[35]

While far from original, this is a fair comment and an apposite one. Assuming that one knows of the existence of certain meaning systems, in Wuthnow's sense of knowing that certain coherent sets of symbols exist in a culture regardless of how individual members of that culture respond to them, the task of discovering whether people find them meaningful is dauntingly complex. As Bainbridge and Stark imply, the analysis of individual sets of responses which lack consistency is so difficult that it is simply not undertaken. But if Wuthnow is correct in saying that an individual can have a 'sense that life is meaningful

– that there is coherence to existence',[36] and also, at the same time, the individual can give an inconsistent set of responses, then the survey researcher (as opposed to the ethnographer) is faced with a problem of analysis which the present author has yet to see solved.

There still remains the problem of identifying extant meaning systems, for the discussion in the previous paragraph was based on the assumption that one does know of their existence. How are they to be identified? I assume that the *ad hoc* method employed in the studies discussed above is inadequate, but that does not imply that no adequate method exists.

A research method

A research method does indeed exist, but it has been used only rarely in the social scientific study of religion. Its first and most distinguished use was in *The Varieties of Religious Experience* by William James. That James was identifying varieties of religious experience rather than varieties of meaning system is immaterial. What is significant is that he delineated certain possible ways in which people do experience religion, and left it to others to study the contemporary prevalence of the experiences he had defined. He did much more in those Gifford Lectures for 1901-2, of course, but he certainly did this. What is instructive for us, I believe, is the data on which James drew for his work, for he was reporting the findings from empirical research, albeit non-quantitative empirical research. The essential point is that he used 'data' in the strictest sense, that is, information which existed already, and which came into existence independently of his own research. How, indeed, one wonders, could it have been otherwise, for he could hardly have based his typology on findings from a survey which asked people about their religious experiences. His sample, while it would perhaps have been random and therefore representative, would not have included the extreme cases of Tolstoy and St Teresa, and yet it is the types he was able to identify from data which included the exotic which throw so much light on the pedestrian experiences of the generality of men and women. His typology has all the qualities which Wuthnow wishes to ascribe to his meaning systems. In particular, his varieties are not categories into which the population may be divided, but 'ideal types' we can use to understand the mundane and inconsistent experience of the population.

A further reason why James could not have proceeded by

using a questionnaire is that he wished to study religious experience as it occurs naturally. For the purposes of an exploratory study, where the ground to be explored is as yet uncharted, one needs to take the evidence as it offers itself. One can properly seek answers to questions only when the appropriate questions are known, and James was aware that he was not in such a position. Placed thus, it is dangerous to ask even loosely phrased and general questions, for the terms of the question will inevitably constrain the answer it receives. The method James adopted was to take documentary material as his data, and in a heuristic study that does appear to be the only satisfactory course of action.

One other well known monograph utilized a similar method. In their study, *Popular Religion*, Louis Schneider and Stanford Dornbusch report the findings of research which analysed documents,[37] and there too it was clearly the appropriate method. There is no more adequate way of discovering what is 'popular' than by surveying patterns of occurrence and consumption. Any question one might ask, such as 'What are your three favourite books?' would elicit answers which are shaped by the respondent's understanding of what the questioner means by 'favourite' and 'books'. To specify 'religious books' would narrow the topic too much, while 'inspirational books' would beg the question. And so on.

My suggestion, then, is that Wuthnow, McCready and Greeley, and Glock and Piazza, should all have begun their work with exploratory empirical studies, for 'What are the extant meaning systems in America?' is a closely similar question to that asked by Schneider and Dornbusch: 'What are the popular religious themes in contemporary America?' Nor is the method untried. The seminal work of Thomas and Znaniecki is not only an exemplary study, but also contains a careful and lengthy methodological note.[38] Following Thomas and Znaniecki, the use of letters for documentary analysis constitutes a useful alternative to published sources, as will become evident below.

The problem

The problem which I shall examine in the remainder of this book is affected by the issues raised in the preceding pages, but it is on a much smaller scale than anything we have considered. Just as one cannot proceed to study religion at the most general and inclusive level of 'meaning systems' without first knowing the range of available 'meaning systems', so, I contend, one cannot

11

study 'conventional religion' unless one first knows the range of ways in which people are 'conventionally religious'. Sociologists generally assume that they have this knowledge, but I dispute the assumption.

We can see the way in which sociologists assume that they know the ways in which people can be religious when they conduct studies of conventional religion by considering two justly influential books from the 1960s. In *Religion and Society in Tension*, Charles Glock and Rodney Stark were able to show that there was wide variation in degrees of religious commitment among the members of various religious denominations in the USA.[39] The methodological innovation they made in that study was to assess religious commitment on the five dimensions of experiential, ritualistic, ideological, intellectual, and consequential, recognizing that people may express commitment in a variety of ways. Looking at their treatment of the ideological dimension, i.e. belief, we see that they were fully aware of the dangers of employing an over-simplified approach. Thus they wrote:

> For the most part, past research has studied religious belief from the standpoint of traditional church doctrine and has asked simply, 'How do people differ with respect to their acceptance of church doctrine?' A number of scales and indexes have been developed, some simple and some complex, whose purpose usually is to order people along a continuum ranging from traditional belief through liberal or modern belief to unbelief. Almost always these measures are conceived in unilateral terms and assume, implicitly at least, that the greater number of beliefs that a subject holds, the stronger is his belief. . . . we should first like to consider the appropriateness of conceiving of religious belief, even traditional belief, in a unilateral way. The failure to make distinctions in kind within the general category of religious belief may obscure some fundamental differences in *types* of belief and *types* of unbelief. . . . Future research will probably reveal the need to develop typologies of religious belief within which degree of religiosity can be measured rather than a single scale of religious commitment on which all individuals can be measured.[40]

The degree of caution they expressed puts them beyond reproach. When one examines the findings from their empirical investigation, however, it is apparent that the discrimination between different types of belief and unbelief has been left for 'future research'. They asked, 'Which of the following statements comes closest to what you believe about God?' and they report the frequencies with which various groups chose one of the following answers:

1 I know God really exists and I have no doubts about it.
2 While I have doubts, I feel that I do believe in God.
3 I find myself believing in God some of the time, but not at other times.
4 I don't believe in a personal God, but I do believe in a higher power of some kind.
5 I don't know whether there is a God and I don't believe there is any way to find out.
6 I don't believe in God.
7 No answer.

Commenting on the distribution of responses, Glock and Stark say, 'it is strikingly apparent that even in a sample of only church members, there are indeed important contrasts both in conceptions of God and in conviction'.[41] In fact only two conceptions are offered, the unqualified 'God' and the 'higher power of some kind', the latter being chosen by 7 per cent of Protestants and 3 per cent of Catholics,[42] and these two 'types' of belief are not given any justification. One is left wondering how many of the respondents who believe in God have in mind a being who is cruel or kind, close at hand or remote, etc.

Glock and Stark, it seems, had the best of intentions and understood the problem, but they proceeded to their survey of the population without first researching the categories they were to employ.

Shortly before this work appeared in print, Gerhard Lenski published *The Religious Factor*.[43] In his research he used two forms of commitment to assess the religiousness of respondents. The first was the commitment of individuals to a socio-religious group, and this was broken down again into 'associational commitment', i.e. involvement in church activities, and 'communal commitment', i.e. restricting the circle of one's friends, and more particularly one's marriage partner, to members of one's own religious group. The second was 'commitment to a type of religious orientation which transcends socio-religious group lines.[44] If we consider Lenski's remarks about this form of commitment we shall see that he too had a clear grasp of the problem to which I have drawn attention:

> To properly assess the influence of religious commitment, it is also necessary to study the influence of different religious orientations. In the religious tradition of the Western world, various types of religious orientations have competed with one

another, each emphasizing a different facet of the Judaic-Christian heritage. Among the more prominent are mysticism, devotionalism, asceticism, ceremonialism, doctrinal orthodoxy, millennialism, and ethicalism. Sometimes individuals emphasize one orientation to the almost total exclusion of the others; sometimes several orientations are cultivated simultaneously. Over the years the relative importance of these orientations has shifted many times as one, then another, gained the ascendancy, but all survive to the present day. . . . In the present study it did not prove practical to investigate the influence of all the many orientations found in the rich and complex Judaic-Christian tradition. Rather we limited our investigation to two orientations which seemed most likely to be related to the problem at hand. These are doctrinal orthodoxy and devotionalism.[45]

Having described the problem of various religious orientations so clearly, Lenski baulks at solving it, preferring to make an *ad hoc* choice. Like Glock and Stark, Lenski recognizes that different types of religiousness obtain among the conventional churches and denominations, but he recognizes it speculatively, and does not examine empirically which types are extant.

We have seen both Glock and Stark and also Lenski state the problem with which I am concerned here, so I do not need to restate it. To distinguish types of conventional religiousness is a parallel task to distinguishing types of invisible religion or meaning system, and it is my belief that the present confusion of those who are studying meaning systems would have been much less if the earlier, and more modest, problem with conventional religion had been tackled, rather than shelved for 'further research' which remains to be undertaken. The findings reported here should go some way to providing a solution to the problem, and the solution may form the basis for more adequate survey work.[46]

The data and the analysis

Aware of the problem outlined above, but before I had formulated it clearly, I was provided with data which are almost ideally suited to solving it. The data came my way more by chance than by design, for I was at a conference at which Dr J. A. T. Robinson, then the Bishop of Woolwich, was also a participant. This was some years after the publication in 1963 of his best-selling religious book *Honest to God*, and I happened to mention that the letters he had received in response to the book, had he kept them, would have been an invaluable source for contemporary religious ideas. To my surprise, he had indeed kept them. To my even greater surprise, he offered to lend them to me. It is on the analysis of those four thousand or so letters that this study is based.

As I had anticipated, the *Honest to God* letters are not about *Honest to God*.[47] A small minority of the people who wrote to Dr Robinson had read the book, and almost all of the letters follow the same format: they make reference to the book (or to a television appearance, or to a printed article referring to the book) in a short sentence or two, and then begin, 'What I believe is . . . .' The book's publication gave rise to public controversy about 'the truth of religion' and it was this controversy, not the book, which prompted people to write with their own opinions – for, as we know, everyone has opinions on religion. The reason the letters came to be written, of course, was that there was a person to whom people could write. To some people he was a villain, to others a man of great courage, to others a person who was at least prepared to have an open mind, but anyone could write to The Bishop of Woolwich, Woolwich, London.

The letters are not from a representative sample of England or any other population, of course. But this did not matter. Like the work of William James, the analysis was to be empirical but not quantitative. My intuitive judgment is that the sample was not notably unrepresentative in respect to either age or sex, but class is another matter, and it is clear that the working class, in particular the young working-class male population, is severely underrepresented.[48]

While a more balanced sample would have been pleasing to analyse, there is no reason to suppose that it would have yielded significantly different results. The reason why this is so is that the letters were not analysed to see what people believed, but what types of religiousness exist. What people write represents a response to the ideas which seem credible or meaningful. None but the tiniest minority in a population works out for himself or for herself a set of ideas: we respond to the available stock of ideas and symbols.[49] What the analysis sought to uncover, therefore, was the set of principal types of religiousness which were extant in the culture from which the letters came, namely Britain, and to a lesser extent the British Commonwealth, the USA and Europe.

The analysis proceeded in two stages. In the first stage, three research assistants and I read photocopies of the letters, marking passages which dealt with identifiable themes, and noting the themes which occurred. After a few hundred letters had been read, the themes recorded thus far were roughly ordered into a catalogue, and the work begun afresh, using the theme numbers from the catalogue to analyse each letter. The analysis continued in this manner, the catalogue being augmented with each new theme which was identified, and letters being analysed by a progressively augmented catalogue of themes. Additions to the catalogue were either ideas encountered for the first time, or sub-types of themes already catalogued. In the many months this analysis took, each letter being read by two researchers independently, the catalogue was revised seven times, and the final version is reproduced as an Appendix at the end of this volume. This first stage was complete when, after somewhat more than half the letters had been analysed, very few additions to the catalogue occurred, for the goal of the analysis was a definitive catalogue rather than a complete set of analysed letters. The remainder of the letters were then read less carefully, and a few additional themes identified and catalogued. We were left with a completed catalogue, analysed letters, and cross-referenced indexes of themes and letters.

I undertook the second stage of the analysis on my own. Perhaps it would be more correct to call it synthesis than analysis, for it entailed the construction of types from the themes scattered through the letters. The method employed was to select all the letters recorded as containing one set of themes (the set of themes relating to Jesus was used), and to sort these letters into the smallest possible number of types of letter, which was nine. The provisional types were not named, but simply left as comparatively discrete types. More letters were selected which shared some theme occurring frequently in letters of one type, and the larger number of letters was re-read, and the coherence of each type reassessed. Piecing types together from large numbers of letters was in no sense rigorously systematic, and having done it myself I could not instruct anyone else in how to complete the task. As weeks passed there were nine, and then seven, piles of letters. The letters in each pile changed, but as they changed the essential character of the pile became clearer. The number of piles was finally reduced to five, and I attempted to characterize each of them, knowing that my characterization of a pile of letters did not capture any one of the letters, let alone the set. They were characterizations of types of religousness, first drafts of the five chapters which follow.

For the benefit of anyone who attempts a similar form of analysis, I should put it on record that the construction of types from primary source material must be a subjective procedure. One or two letters, at most six or seven, emerge as being quintessential of a type, but they will rarely conform wholly to the type and they will never illustrate every facet of it. These quintessential documents are nevertheless of the greatest importance. They have the same significance that certain cases had for William James. A type requires much more than a few such cases, however, for it must be built up to have a coherence of its own, and in order to round out the picture one must be prepared to take fragments from many documents.

The types described here are 'ideal-types' in Weber's sense of the term.[50] They are not categories. They have the strengths and the weaknesses of ideal types, for they have considerable analytic power and yet are of little immediate utility in quantitative empirical research. Thus they will help in the construction of a survey instrument by alerting a researcher to crucial items which should not be omitted although of little intrinsic interest, but they cannot be taken as guides, still less as blue-prints, for drawing up a questionnaire. They are more obviously useful in the interpretation of survey results, but again their usefulness is not immediate for they point to appropriate methods of interpretation rather than to interpretations *per se*. I include a few remarks at the end of each chapter about the way in which a type may be discerned in survey data, but we shall return to the problem in the final chapter.

The passages from letters which are quoted for illustration have been altered as little as possible, but where necessary personal details have been changed to ensure anonymity, and misspellings and badly defective grammar have generally been corrected. In general I have attempted to follow Durkheim's dictum in presenting these types:

> Let him experience it as the believer experiences it, for it really only exists in virtue of what it is for the latter. Thus whoever does not bring to the study of religion a sort of religious sentiment has no right to speak about it![51]

And the reader is invited to adopt the same attitude of mind. It would be easy to caricature these types, but I have endeavoured to do the opposite, and to portray each as a comprehensible and credible way of being religious. For this reason I hope that anyone who should recognize his or her own words quoted here will not be displeased. People wrote to Dr Robinson because they had opinions and wished to express them. If they were fairly represented, as I hope they are, those opinions will gain wider circulation by being reproduced here.

Most of the letters analysed in this research were written nearly twenty years ago, but while certain facts and turns of phrase make them into period pieces, they are not dated. The types of religion described here change very slowly indeed, and even their popularity is stable. My model, in some respects, is William James and I take heart from the fact that *The Varieties of Religious Experience* has dated hardly at all.

To repeat the point made at the beginning of this chapter, the types portrayed here are types of conventional religiousness. People representative of the types might be found in the same church next Sunday, and if they are different from one another they are unaware of the degree of difference. Sociologists of religion, however, should know of the differences, and conduct their research accordingly.

2 Exemplarism

The first type of religiousness to be examined is focussed on the man Jesus. I call it *exemplarism* because it sees in Jesus, in his life and death, and in his teaching, an example for all to follow.

In order to understand this type of religiousness we shall need to grasp two things: firstly, the nature of the example which Jesus is seen to offer; and secondly, what beliefs, experiences and practices are associated with a focus on Jesus as the compelling example for human life.

Exemplarism has been an element in Christianity throughout its history, and in view of the invitation of Jesus to his disciples to 'Follow me', it could not have been otherwise. Weber distinguished between exemplary prophets and ethical prophets, giving the Buddha as an example of the former, and Zoroaster and Mohammed as examples of the latter,[1] and while it is true that Christians have always sought to follow the teachings of Jesus this aspect of discipleship has never eclipsed the desire to imitate him and to follow the pattern of his life. But if Jesus has always been an exemplar for Christians it has not always been the same Jesus who has been followed, for the image of Jesus has undergone radical changes over the centuries. The history of those transformations is part of that branch of theology called Christology, and while it is unnecessary to trace that history here we must note two important antecedents of the exemplarism which occurs in the twentieth century.[2] The first is the teaching of the twelfth-century philosopher and theologian Peter Abelard.[3] While Abelard's views affected few people at the time they are interesting in the present context because they included the idea that the suffering of Christ was a supreme example, and little more. This theory of the atonement, which is known as exemplarism, was in sharp contrast to the theory generally

19

accepted at the time, according to which the death of Christ was an efficacious event in a wholly objective sense, since it defeated the powers of evil throughout the cosmos. In Abelard's view it was subjectively effective, and the implication of this view is that the humanity of Christ and his human example are accorded pre-eminent importance.

The second antecedent of contemporary exemplarism is much closer to our own time, and indeed could be said to be not an antecedent at all, but the event which inaugurated this type of religiousness as it is found today. Ernest Renan, like Abelard a Frenchman, published *The Life of Christ* in 1863. It was not the first biography of Jesus to appear in the nineteenth century, for *The Life of Jesus* by D.F. Strauss was published nearly thirty years earlier, and nor was the idea of a biography of Jesus unusual, for the genre flourished in the last century, but it was of incomparable importance. As Owen Chadwick has written, the book

> was unique, because it appeared at a unique moment of time, late enought for the learned world to begin the quest for the historical Jesus and move towards the idea of biography, early enough for the world not to have seen that the quest could not result in that kind of biography. . . . It was the most famous book written in France during the nineteenth century.[4]

Renan viewed Jesus as an inspired genius and as someone who transformed human society, but he regarded everything super-natural in the gospel stories as primitive superstitions of an earlier age, and therefore the portrait he painted was of a 'beautiful and original and self-sacrificial genius of ethical understanding, who by the union between moral person and moral teaching changed the world'.[5] Like the exemplarists of today, Renan worshipped Jesus. But like today's exemplarists he believed the supernatural trappings of the story, originally the grounds of faith, to be the main obstacle to faith in Jesus now: 'If ever the worship of Jesus loses its hold upon mankind, it will be precisely on account of those acts which originally inspired belief in him.'[6] It is important to notice that Renan worshipped Jesus; that he was a religious man; that his apparent irreligion was prompted by religious motives. He imagined Christ saying to him, 'You must leave me if you would be my disciple.'[7] Renan left the Catholic Church in 1845 but he was a religious person in a sense in which Comte, who founded a religion, was not, and it is important to recognize that the views which compelled Renan to leave the Church came slowly, via the Modernist controversies of the turn of the century, to be not unusual among people who remained in the Church.[8] Private judgment, the error which more than any other Pius X sought to stamp out, has become a religious imperative even in the Church of Rome.[9]

What I want to emphasize by referring to Peter Abelard and Ernest Renan is that exemplarism, a type of religiousness which denies much of the traditional Christian religion in order that it may honour the man Jesus, is neither new nor un-religious. It has been an element in Christianity throughout its history, and while the champions of exemplarism have often been tried for heresy their motives have always been profoundly religious. A contemporary example is Don Cupitt[10] who has taken the title of one of his recent books from a remark of the German Dominican mystic, Meister Eckhart (1260-1327): 'Man's last and highest parting occurs when, for God's sake, he takes leave of God.' In that book Cupitt argues that Christians should part company with the thought of an objective God, and struggle to realize religious values in this life, in relation to prevailing social and economic conditions, on the grounds that nothing else is available. The type of religiousness which Cupitt advocates is not very different from that represented by Renan a hundred years ago. Nor does it depart in spirit from the religious vision of Eckhart or Abelard many hundreds of years ago.

All is not exactly the same, however, and one might argue that exemplarism has a popular appeal today whereas it was a vision exclusive to a few exceptional individuals in former ages. That argument could be advanced quite convincingly, I believe, by reference to Lionel Trilling's account of the transition from the rule of sincerity to the dominance of authenticity.[11] The rise in popularity of exemplarism from the period of Ernest Renan might, furthermore, add weight to the thesis which Richard Sennett expounds in *The Fall of Public Man*.[12] But I am not concerned with popularity. In this chapter I shall merely describe a type of religiousness which is extant today, without reference to the extent of its prevalence.

If it has been a different Jesus who has caught the imagination of successive generations, who is the Jesus who commands attention in the latter part of the twentieth century? Those whom I describe as exemplarists, that is those whose whole religion is dominated by the figure of Jesus, are no longer moved by the gentle teacher from Galilee. Nor are they stirred by the 'Light of the World' as depicted by Holman Hunt. If one were looking for a visual representation it might be 'Christ of St John of the Cross' by Dali, or Epstein's 'Christ in Majesty' in Llandaff Cathedral. It is isolation and aloneness which characterize the contemporary Jesus. Today he is the solitary hero, the twentieth-century heir of

Siegfried and Tristan. In the orthodox Christian tradition Jesus was prefigured in Moses and David, themselves the heroes of Judaism, but the heroic figure of Jesus has recently been subject to the same transformation as one finds in novels of the twentieth century. The modern hero is no longer the victor who triumphed against enormous odds, splendidly arrayed and surrounded by the corpses of the thousands he has slain, like Wellington or Napoleon. It may be the experience of modern war or of modern society in general, but the dramatic shift in emphasis finds today's hero the winner of a very private and unspectacular victory. The Jesus who appeals to the contemporary imagination was a good man who got what life gives to good men. He was, as one letter put it:

> that man who put his shoulder to the wheel in order to turn the world, and who found that it crushed him. It is precisely because the world is for the rich and the strong and the powerful, and that there is no other, that I can see his commitment so clearly, and try to identify myself with it. (2298)

Such is the contemporary figure of Jesus, and the central feature of exemplarism as a type of religiousness is the way it focuses attention on the man Jesus as an example to be followed.

As we shall see, exemplarism is indeed heroic, and heroic in a sophisticated way, but the same low-key heroism appeals also to those who may seem to be unsophisticated, and it is arguable that, in Britain at least, this type of religiousness has an immediate appeal to working-class people. We tend to think of British empiricism as a school of philosophy, forgetting that empiricism and pragmatism are deeply ingrained as a way of approaching the whole of life which is as characteristic of the British attitude to religion as to much else. Thus Richard Hoggart, in his book on British working-class culture, *The Uses of Literacy*, can write:

> Christianity is morals; [the phrase] 'Christ's teaching', is the one most commonly heard when the talk is in favour of religion. Christ was a person, giving the best example of how to live; one could not be expected to live like that today; still, the example is there.[13]

'Moral', as a concept, is as native to Britain as 'spiritual' is foreign, and exemplarism is a moral type of religiousness. Those who are confirmed non-church-goers and yet who revere the life and teaching of Jesus, saying that you do not have to go to church to be a Christian and that they have their own religion, are not merely lazy or self-excusing, as church-goers sometimes self-righteously suppose. They are telling the truth. It is a religion which is learned at home, articulated in clubs and pubs and works canteens, and embodied in working-class institutions such as Christmas clubs, friendly societies and trade unions. Since we are concerned to understand religion as people themselves understand it, let us consider a further passage from *The Uses of Literacy* which can stand as one definition among others.

> Here, round the sense of religion as a guide to our duty
> towards others, as the repository of good rules for communal
> life, the old phrases cluster. Ask any half-dozen working-class
> people what they understand by religion, and very easily, but
> not meaninglessly, they will be likely to answer with one of
> these phrases:
> 'doing good',
> 'common decency',
> 'helping lame dogs',
> 'being kind',
> 'doing unto others as y'would be done unto',
> 'we're 'ere to 'elp one another',
> ''elping y'neighbour',
> 'learning to know right from wrong',
> 'decent living'.
> . . . 'Ah like fair dealings' may seem an inadequate guide
> to the cosmos and can be self-righteous, but – said sincerely by
> a middle-aged man after a hard life – it can represent a
> considerable triumph over difficult circumstances.[14]

Hoggart was writing about those who for the most part are unchurched, and who are without a trace of guilt about it. They are also unlikely to write letters to bishops. The exemplarist religion of working-class people is undifferentiated from the rest of working-class culture because it is unchurched,[15] but since a survey of religion is bound to include many working-class respondents, the continuities between the sophisticated and self-conscious exemplarism described here, and working-class exemplarism must not be overlooked.

The Christ of exemplarism, then, is a hero. He is the man who lived a good life and whom men should strive to emulate. Something more about this modern hero will become clear as we proceed, but let us now consider some of the attitudes and beliefs which go together to make up exemplarism as a type of religiousness.

We have seen that there is a working-class exemplarism which is simply unchurched, but that is no more than the limiting case, for exemplarists always find it hard to come to terms with the Church. In so far as the personal example of Jesus constitutes the core of a religious attitude, the Church, as the institution organized in his name, can never be important. Indeed it can easily be seen as an obstacle to belief, for the personal, charismatic authority of Jesus is incompatible with the authority of an institution which is bound to make essentially institutional demands on its members to ensure its own survival as a healthy institution.[16] Because the idea of 'being a Christian' is so commonly thought to entail belonging to the Church and accepting its teachings, exemplarists inevitably feel that they are heretics and outsiders, despite being disciples of Jesus. They may feel obliged to join the Church because, at least in name, it is the group of Jesus's declared followers; they may be church-goers who survive the experience only by having a great number of mental reservations about the Church's teachings; they may feel that they have been driven out of the Church because Church membership positively obstructs commitment to the example of Jesus; or they may not even regard church-going as an option worth considering. Whether it is adopted reluctantly or with defiance, however, the exemplarist's attitude to the Church is at best critical, at worst clearly negative. The following range of responses to the Church and its teachings are characteristic of this attitude. An elderly woman wrote:

> I belonged to no church until, two years ago, I was confirmed and entered the Anglican community. My fundamental reason was (I *think*, though it is extremely difficult to analyse and be sure) that I could ignore Christ no longer and felt obliged to make a definite step towards him. (666)

This reluctant, 'I can no other', attitude is as near as exemplarism can come to a positive response. It stems from the need to make a public action which will express a private conviction. A less positive attitude is seen in those who doggedly go on as Church members while finding themselves disappointed and disillusioned by the Church, and while understanding all too well why others do not. Thus another woman, of a similar age, wrote that she and her friends

> do believe that Christ was the way and the life, in that he gave us the key to living – Love. So simple and sure. Many do not go to church because they cannot accept the virgin birth or other doctrines, even on the basis of 'thought forms' of the time. Yet they live as Christians. And religion is a way of living. As a widow I have found church-going the loneliest part

of widowhood. I found 90% of those in church were not
Christ-like. (2430)

Another way of being negative is to be aloof, participating in
Church activities and Church services but consciously placing
upon them one's own private meaning. The following passage
from a letter from a man illustrates this cavalier approach to the
Church. The negative attitude to the Church is entirely
characteristic of exemplarism; the references to God are not,
since the exemplarist finds meaning only in the man Jesus, as we
shall see below.

> I met a lady the other day who had been born and brought up
> a Roman Catholic. She told me she had left the Roman
> Church. She said, 'No, I don't belong to anyone now, you see
> I am not prepared to allow any religion to come between me
> and my God.' I had not put it to myself in that way but I think
> that must be largely my own attitude. . . . I regard the
> teachings of Jesus Christ as of divine origin and therefore they
> must be accepted without question or argument. The liturgy
> and all the rest I regard as man-made, to be accepted or
> rejected in accordance with one's own judgement. That
> enables me to enjoy corporate worship in a Church as I simply
> do not join in any part of the service which I do not believe in
> or understand. (1764)

The more thorough-going rejection which Ernest Renan felt
obliged to make is still a typical reaction for the exemplarist. As
the Church, even the Roman Catholic Church, has lost its
magisterial power the exemplarist feels free quietly to slip away
without public fuss or inner struggle. The power has not gone
altogether, though, and so an exemplarist may well experience
his or her rejection of the Church as something traumatic, as we
see in a letter from another man:

> I am a convinced and I hope a practising Christian, and I
> accept Christ's message and His ethics as being quite the finest
> way of life ever conceived for mankind. None the less I found
> when I reached adult status that attendance at church was
> becoming too great a strain upon my personal honesty, and
> too great an embarrassment because of what I began to feel
> was a false image superimposed many years ago and totally
> out of place in a more sophisticated twentieth century. I just
> could not bring myself to sing hymns and recite prayers which
> reflected this false image, and in the end I stayed away. . . . I
> *wish* that I could once again believe what as a little child I
> believed implicitly and unquestioningly. Instead I find that

> Christmas-time is sullied by the insistence that Christ's birth
> was magical. Once upon a time the Virgin Birth would have
> been a reason for belief. To me, and I must say to my infinite
> regret, it is a stumbling block. A reason for UNBELIEF. (214)

The religion of the exemplarist is a private affair. So far from relying on the support of the Church and its teaching, exemplarism finds the Church an impediment to belief in Jesus. Jesus himself is an example, and his example gives a lead to those who are prepared to follow; it powerfully inspires in the way that only a hero can inspire. It is more than the example of a good life, however, for it has the singular properties of the supreme hero, but for whose example we should have neither a model to follow nor the courage to follow it. The heroism of Jesus which inspires people today consists, as I have suggested already, in a moral stature which is unadorned by any obvious success. It is nearer to the ideal which Dag Hammarskjöld set for himself: 'Only one feat is possible – not to have run away.' There is no success to win admiration beyond the success of fighting never to give in. One letter expresses the achievement of Jesus thus: 'He braved the worst his enemies could do to him and, by the strength of his fighting spirit, lived and thus cheated them.' (2907) But the qualities of Jesus which command the allegiance of exemplarists become fully clear only when we consider what he was not; the parts of the traditional Christian faith rejected by exemplarism tell us as much about it as a religious attitude as do the things affirmed.

Exemplarism does not believe in God or in the life after death, in sin or in salvation. In order to affirm Jesus as the example for human living it has to deny the whole supernatural realm, or at least to be agnostic about it. When the exemplarist turns away from the Church it is because the Church teaches that Jesus is not only the supreme human example, but the principal actor in a cosmic drama. The universal battle between God, on the one hand, and the devil and all his works on the other, has no part in the exemplarist's creed, for his religion is a religion of humanity. Jesus appears as the pinnacle of human aspiration, not as the link between the human and the divine. This is why the exemplarist is so chary of the Church and its teachings about Jesus as God incarnate who came down to wrest man from sin, and the world from Satan.

The woman who was quoted above as saying that she joined the Anglican Church because she 'could ignore Christ no longer' went on to say: 'But I have always felt, in a dim sort of way, that a magnified and more exalted version of Christ, i.e. God, was both unnecessary and unreal.' (666) The same idea is expressed more trenchantly in another letter:

> To acknowledge the existence of any entity outside ourselves, any God who would go on existing if the whole of mankind were wiped out tomorrow is to detract from the potential stature of man. The value of the life of Christ, it seems to me, lies in the fact that he came nearer to being perfect man than any other person, that *God* is perfect man, and that Jesus achieved this perfection without any supernatural aid, without the help of some outside being. (814)

This is the heart of exemplarism, a style of religiousness which has 'taken leave of God'. It would be misleading to call it Christian atheism, for that phrase suggests a strident denial of the existence of God. It would be equally misleading to call it Christian agnosticism, for that suggests that the exemplarist is exercised by the question of whether or not there is a God but has concluded that one cannot know. Exemplarism finds the idea of God 'unnecessary and unreal', and is convinced that to postulate a God robs the Christian religion of its true significance. The language of divinity is used, but it is used as a metaphor to express the nobility of the Christian aspiration. The notion of transcendence, too, has a place in exemplarism, for no other notion can convey the transition from the savage to the saint which is exemplified in the human self-transcendence of Jesus. In Durkheim's sense of the term, the example of Jesus is sacred.

One need hardly say that a Christian denial of God seems strange at first sight, since on any reckoning the man Jesus must have believed in the God of his fathers. So on the one hand a Christianity without God seems peculiar. On the other hand the view is understandable as a development of certain trends in Christianity. It is only in the violently monotheistic religions like Islam that belief in a single sovereign God has survived, and in attributing divinity to Jesus, Christianity opened the way to beliefs which, in their developed forms in both the Eastern and the Western Churches, embraced a concept of the divine diverse enough to rival Hinduism. Catholic theology may never in theory have departed from belief in one God, but the place accorded first to Christ, then to the Blessed Virgin, and then to saints, shrines, relics – and the sacraments, in practice – rendered the One God, the Alpha and Omega, more or less otiose in popular religion. Despite the efforts of Calvinism to reinstate the wholly transcendent God to the position he had occupied in Judaism, as medieval magic declined the form of post-Reformation Christianity which fired popular Protestant enthusiasm focused principally on Christ. By the beginning of the present century children were being taught by devout parents to ask themselves, 'What would Jesus do?' when faced with moral choices, as though he were the epitome of conformism. So when belief in God receded it left Jesus as the model of moral behaviour.

Exemplarism emerges, therefore, as a Christian form of humanism; it is a natural development in a humanistic age of Jesus-centred Christianity, with all the characteristics of humanism. It is Christian because it finds the supreme example of humanity in Christ. As was said above, one of the main problems which exemplarism finds with the Church's teaching is that in claiming that Jesus was divine it compromises his humanity, and for exemplarism his humanity must be complete and unadulterated. A divine Jesus is useless as a human example: if, as one letter put it, 'we have a man who is also God, then he always has a "head start" as it were and can't help doing what is right'. (2295) Unless the exemplarist's hero is like him or her in every respect the hero cannot be a source of realistic hope: 'What we crave is a real man with deep imperfections who can yet finally triumph over himself as proof to each one of us that we may triumph over ourselves.' (2907) Or again: 'A man without sin cannot understand sinners; a man without violent and potentially dangerous passions cannot understand passion.' (2907)

The orthodox account of Christ says that unless he was God he could not have saved the world from sin and reconciled it to God. Exemplarism knows nothing of the problem of a fallen world, and therefore has no need of a solution to the problem. It sees the world as natural and evolving, not fallen from a state of original perfection. Likewise, if men and women are weak, wilful and vicious, that is because they are still progressing towards perfection. Exemplarism, therefore, has no theodicy, no account of how evil and suffering can be allowed by a good God. Confronted with pain, the exemplarist seeks to bear it: one defeats evil by not being defeated by it. When the pain is another's rather than one's own, one hopes that the other will win a similar victory. The model is Promethean, but the inspiration and the courage are drawn from a real person and not from myth. Evil in general does not exist for the exemplarist: it exists only in individual confrontations, for which Jesus is the peerless example. The only general statement the exemplarist will allow is that humanity is slowly progressing towards a state where men and women, without illusions, will all strive to follow the example of Jesus.

The humanistic idea of a perfectible humanity is central to

exemplarism. It sees the whole realm of nature in exclusively natural terms. Impressed by the scientific doctrine of evolution, it sees humanity in an evolutionary perspective, progressing from stupid weakness towards intelligent control of the environment, from ignorance and superstition towards a rational understanding of life. Christianity has great potential for good in the eyes of the exemplarist because it is rooted in the human ideal of Christ. In order to exploit its potential, however, Christianity must shed the metaphysical ideas of a supernatural order impinging on the world. The example of Jesus shows what a person can hope to become, and his teachings speak of a new order of society to which we can aspire. The exemplarist can tolerate the traditional language of Christianity, but only if it is interpreted in a naturalistic way so that the myths are seen as metaphors which convey natural truths. Sin is the imperfection which remains to be transcended; evil is the continued absence of good, not a power in its own right; Christ saves by the example he gives. What is looked for, in the words of one letter, is:

> a steady change in the world, so that love for one's fellow man becomes more dominant and greater harmony is achieved. Individually we contribute to this plan by creating goodness, and through endowing our children with the capacity to carry this on, 'To make this world a better place and life a worthier thing.' (1775)

The role of Christ is clear: 'The Life of Christ is everything to me and not his death on the Cross, and I feel that my salvation depends on the extent to which I practise his Way – the Way of Life.' (45) It is equally clear, however, that much of Christianity tends to block this vision:

> I want nothing to do with a faith which is merely an expression of Man's weakness or Man's need. I believe in the real world, the world of science and experiment, of measurement and observation. I believe in mathematical truth and logical argument and precise thought. I believe in people, in love, and in generosity. And I believe in the Man Jesus. I cannot believe the doctrines associated with the Fall, the Atonement, the Trinity, as they were presented to me. (2408)

Of these doctrines, someone else can write:

> Good in their time they no longer serve their original purposes. Rather do they defeat them. Once upon a time it was good psychology to put across religion in terms of magic.

> Nowadays it is disastrous because intelligent people just don't believe it. (214)

Christianity, for the exemplarist, is a celebration of the hope which Christ inspires of heaven on earth. The difficulty of the struggle which lies ahead and the sufferings which a follower of Christ must expect are not minimized, but the exemplarist's gaze is fixed on what lies beyond. Determined not to be beaten, the exemplarist may be an immediate pessimist, but he or she is an ultimate optimist.

Exemplarism finds hope for the good life in the example of Jesus, but it is important to note that 'hoping' itself is of central significance for this type of religious attitude. It is significant because it captures what I would call the 'cognitive style' of exemplarism.[17] In order to see what is meant here by a cognitive style, consider the following remarks of Rodney Needham:

> Whereas ethnographers, in particular, have become alert to the dangers of denotative terms such as 'soul', 'gift', 'family', and so on, they have continued in the main to adhere uncritically to a received philosophy of mind, namely that provided by the categories of European languages and the prevailing 'tone of thought' that these express. They recognize that culture is differentiated, but they conduct their investigations as though the operation of the mind were undifferentiated. That is, they take it for granted (or at least write as though they took it for granted) that human nature is already adequately charted and determined, so that an ethnographer approaching a foreign culture, or an analyst interpreting published reports, can assume that the human beings under consideration will have certain well-known logical and psychic capacities that they share with the observer. . . . The specific argument of the investigation that I have undertaken here is that the notion of belief is not appropriate to an empirical philosophy of mind or to an exact account of human motives and conduct. Belief is not discriminable experience, it does not constitute a natural resemblance among men, and it does not belong to 'the common behaviour of mankind'.
>
> It follows from this that *when other peoples are said, without qualification, to 'believe' anything*, it must be entirely unclear what kind of idea or state of mind is being ascribed to them. The task of ethnography is to render accurate reports of alien modes of experience, but I cannot find that this has yet been done with respect to belief.[18]

Needham is undoubtedly correct to say that we should be

careful when we attribute 'believing' anything to *other peoples*, but for sociologists studying their own contemporary culture there is an additional problem, or rather there is the same problem under heavier disguise. Who are *we*, and what is *our* culture? My contention is that the 'received philosophy of mind' to which Needham refers belongs to a tiny, intensively socialized, intellectual minority, and that those of us who belong to it should exercise no less caution when studying our fellow-citizens than when we study a 'foreign culture'. We are aware that not all Americans believe the same things, and that not all Britons believe the same things; we must become alert to the fact that not all Americans mean the same thing when they say that they 'believe' something, and that Britons are in the same predicament. Two professional philosophers, one a member of the Plymouth Brethren and the other a member of the Divine Light Mission, will be able to discuss 'belief' by drawing on a received philosophy of mind which they share as professional philosophers, but they will employ the word differently when they are in their respective sectarian milieux.[19]

By 'cognitive style' I shall mean that version of 'belief' which is part of a distinctive style of religiousness. When exemplarists use the word 'believe', as in the utterance, 'Lord I believe, help thou mine unbelief', we understand their meaning best if we take them to have said, 'Lord I hope, may my hope not fail'. Hope for exemplarism is more than the substance of its aspirations: it is the cognitive style of exemplarism as a form of religiousness. Exemplarism is orientated to a better future, and it dares to hope for that future because if focuses its attention on the achievement of Jesus as an example of what humanity is capable of becoming. Exemplarism is concerned with the possibilities of human achievement; it hopes for a continually improving world, and it finds in Jesus both the embodiment of what is hoped for and also the courage to hope for it. It is unlike traditional Christianity because it is not concerned with the supernatural, nor with the cosmic epic of the world's creation out of nothing by God, with its fall as a result of Adam's sin, and its rescue from the power of Satan by the sacrifice on the cross of God-made-man. Exemplarists do indeed see life in terms of an epic struggle, but the epic is played out by men and women, and only on the stage of this earth. They find wholly unappealing the larger image of the cosmic forces of Good and Evil meeting on Calvary, where Good vanquished Evil and so made its victorious power available to men and women down to the present day. If exemplarists want such an epic myth they will, if they are young, perhaps immerse themselves in the story of the fight against the Dark Lord in

31

Tolkien's *Lord of the Rings*; if they are older they may be lovers of Wagner or read stories of the Second World War. The Christian myth, however, is not to their taste. They want their religion to restrict itself to the human drama of life and love and death in the realm of hard fact.

The rejection of the Christian myth is not necessarily simple or without pain, but evokes as wide a range of responses as the negative attitude to the Church described earlier. One young man preparing for ordination to the ministry of the Church of England had accepted the advice he had been given while struggling with his doubts,

> that if one was able to affirm the centrality of Jesus, even if one couldn't go on to make metaphysical statements about God, then it was 'alright' so to speak. . . . Perhaps we should just try and follow Jesus and not worry about the rest. (2385)

The rejection of the myth, of the metaphysical, does constitute a distinctive and distinctively different style of religion. The young man whose letter has just been quoted would achieve an amazingly low score on a standard religiosity scale. A style of religiousness which sees in the life of Jesus a sacred model for human living but which eschews belief in God, in sin, in a fallen creation, in the redemption of the world, and in divine grace, is a long way from the Christian norm.

Other beliefs besides these are unacceptable to exemplarists, and two in particular merit attention. In keeping with their dislike of speculation about the metaphysical and the unknown, exemplarists do not believe in a life after death. When they pray, 'Thy kingdom come', they are giving expression to the hope that a new order of society may be created in which men and women will live Christ-like lives, and from which fear and injustice, ignorance and greed will be banished. As one letter put it: 'the riches of Christ are not to be found in "Gloryland up there" but in "slumberland down here".' (1916) This is not to say that the *vita venturi saeculi*, the life of the world to come, means nothing to the exemplarist. Clearly, life goes on, and the exemplarist asks what kind of life, and where, should be hoped for. In answer to these questions the exemplarist may say:

> I see the life hereafter as the continuance of the good which I have created in the world, and the good in me being carried on through the good in my children and those whom I have been able to help. (1775)

Exemplarism puzzles over these questions. It assumes that belief in the life to come must be sensible, that there must be such a thing, for the followers of Jesus have asserted it for two thousand years. What it rejects in the idea conveyed by the familiar phrase, 'the after-life'. So the exemplarist will seek the true meaning of the belief, and may suggest:

> The doctrine is (biblically) a qualitative assertion about the present (life of infinite value), not a quantitative assertion about the future (life of infinite length). In a word, nothing happens after death, except the obvious. (2571)

Naturally, the question of the life of the world to come is not only a matter of individual survival. It is connected with the belief that Jesus 'rose from the dead', and the ultimate fate of Jesus is inseparable from the ultimate fate of those who follow his example. Thus another person can write:

> I have even come to wonder whether the true meaning of Christ's victory over death was not, and is not, the survival of his message and his influence, rather than his person. . . . Is it not more consistent with man's dignity to live without hopes of eternity? Or is this merely Promethean pride? My favourite quotation from Shakespeare –
>
> > Things won are done;
> > Joy's soul lies in the doing –
>
> is an argument for 'soldiering on', not for living on expectation. (1821)

The expectation of a life beyond the grave in which good done on earth will receive its reward and ill its punishment, however, is absent from the exemplarist's faith. Life is here and now or not at all; he or she looks forward to a day when the world is a better place in which to live because people have heeded the teaching of Christ and used to the full the intelligence with which they are naturally endowed.

Exemplarism is hardly a revolutionary creed, but neither is it a conservative one. Its doctrine of human nature is a high one, verging on the Promethean, which makes it the very opposite of Sigmund Freud's idea of religion as something rooted in guilt and dependence, serving effectively to perpetuate guilt and dependence. Conceiving the natural order to be essentially beneficent, marred only by its imperfect development, exemplarism looks forward to a continued progress not unlike the progress towards Omega Point which was plotted by Teilhard de Chardin in *The Phenomenon of Man*. The advent of Jesus Christ marked a decisive stage in the progress because the example of his life provided a unique insight into potential human stature. Another important point was passed but recently, for humanity has now shaken itself free of the supernatural myth, and knowing that they stand alone, men and women are able to follow the example of Jesus with a new realism and with added resolution. So exemplarism has none of the soporific effects of a religion which directs the attention away from this world towards one beyond the grave where we can expect compensation for present deprivations; since this world is the only one there is, it is the place for action.

It is clear that exemplarism represents an adaptation of traditional Christian ideas to an age which finds it difficult to accept concepts of the supernatural. One could go on to argue that it is a religious response to a culture in which external authority is intrinsically suspect. A religion which focuses on a human example is peculiarly well adapted to an age in which the supreme value is human authenticity, for only a human voice is able to speak authoritatively to those for whom the human individual is sovereign. Following Durkheim, the sociological perspective can see it as more than a coincidence that the declining authority of social groups, and of society in general, should go hand in hand with the declining plausibility of supernatural conceptions: exemplarism appears as an adaptation of Christianity to the sensibilities of the lonely crowd.[20] But it is a religious reaction to changes which have taken place in secular culture. It is not like the Anabaptist sects in the sixteenth century or the various puritan sects at the time of the English Civil War whose doctrines were genuine religious innovations, or at the least cultural innovations which could be articulated only in terms of religious doctrine. Those religious movements had profound effects on secular culture, while exemplarism represents a religious adaptation to secular culture.[21] The ineffectiveness of exemplarism derives from its low doctrine of the Church, for only a style of religiousness which attaches positive significance to the social group of the believers can have an effect on society. Exemplarism is too individualistic a form of religiousness, too akin to existentialist and psycho-analytic movements in philosophy, to represent any kind of radical challenge to the existing social order. If, on the one hand, exemplarists are not lulled into accepting present ills, on the other hand their religion does not provide them with any hope of a better future which is not equally accessible to secular humanists. Its strength lies in its use of a religious vocabulary and its appeal to the example of Jesus. But it could be argued that that strength is largely sapped by its struggle with the more conservative forms of religiousness.

'Thy kingdom come', it has been suggested, is a prayer which gives expression to the hope of a new order of society in which men and women will lead Christ-like lives, but the very act of praying is itself problematical for exemplarists, and this brings us to the second belief which is unacceptable to exemplarism that merits special mention. Exemplarists do not believe in prayer. When they pray, as pray they must if they go to church, they conceive of what they are doing as some kind of process of self-conditioning whereby they come to a conscious realization of their place in the universe and of their proper relation to their fellow human beings. In so far as exemplarists pray on their own, solitarily, they are attempting to bring the example of Jesus more fully to mind and to examine their own lives in the light of that example. For the most part, however, the exemplarist will consider that one's time is better spent in actively living a Christ-like life than in contemplating it. They know that prayer can avoid the idea of someone, or something, being prayed to only with the greatest difficulty, and talk about God is dangerous. All too easily it places exemplarists on the slippery slope which leads them back to a sub-human mentality of dependence and supplication, and it is precisely that frame of mind from which they seek to struggle free. The idea of intercessory prayer, of asking God for what is needed by oneself or by others, is plainly unacceptable since it implies a power which intervenes in the natural processes of the world, but any kind of prayer is potentially dangerous. A man who was trying to come to terms with the problems raised by prayer wrote:

> We don't want either of our boys to be indoctrinated with ideas of God who looks after boys and girls and will make them good and truthful if they ask. Truth and goodness must be their responsibility against the background of our love. . . . My wife has the good fortune of being able to meditate for long periods, and that without any training. She dwells at depth. She tells me she never thinks of addressing some exalted, far-away Being. So is it enough to content ourselves with Jesus 'our hero strong and tender'? If we are going to drop the logically odd word 'God' let's do it from the word go and spare our children the agonies of unlearning pious language. (2558)

Prayer must be radically re-interpreted if it is to be acceptable to the exemplarist.

Exemplarism is a type of religiousness which focuses exclusively on the life and message of Jesus. The Church and its teachings about the supernatural are at best irrelevancies against

35

which exemplarists must guard in order to avoid polluting their simple hope of following in the Master's footsteps; at worst they are an evil to be avoided at all costs, since 'being a Christian' is a matter for individuals to work at on their own without the distractions of a religious club which is the hangover from an earlier age.

If this style of religiousness is heterodox, and if there is no club or organization for those who embrace it, then how and why does it survive? I will offer four broad reasons.

Firstly, there are those people, church-goers from birth or from adolescence, who run into intellectual difficulties in adult life and who seek an interpretation of their religion which is consistent with the secular culture, which they take for granted. Exemplarism survives, in other words, because it is a style of religiousness which is compatible with the beliefs and values of western societies: science, individualism, bourgeois liberalism, etc. While people still find themselves Christians without having made a mature and self-conscious decision, this reason is likely to remain effective.

Secondly, exemplarism survives because it is one part of the Christianity taught by the Church. Moralizing sermons frequently refer the people in the pews to the example of Jesus 'our hero strong and tender', and the conventional hymnology is replete with Christocentric verses of varying degrees of sentimentality. The formal teaching and liturgy of the Church, too, contains an important element of exemplarism. Thus, for example, the evening hymn which has traditionally been sung in the week before Easter begins with the verse:

> The royal banners forward go;
> The Cross shines forth in mystic glow;
> Where he in flesh, our flesh who made,
> Our sentence bore, our ransom paid;

But the collect, or appointed prayer, runs thus:

> Almighty and everlasting God, who, by thy tender love
> towards mankind, has sent thy Son, our Saviour Jesus Christ,
> to take upon him our flesh, and to suffer death upon the cross,
> that all mankind should follow the example of his great
> humility: Mercifully grant, that we may both follow the
> example of his patience, and also be made partakers of his
> resurrection.

The prayer is entirely acceptable to the exemplarist, who will make allowances for the hymn on the grounds that it was written in the sixth or seventh century.

Thirdly, organizations exist, within the Church of England for example, which are exemplarist in tone if not in intent. They are not overtly religious, but they are religious in origin and they serve to keep people in touch with the Church. The Scout Association, for example, which was founded in 1908, exists 'to encourage the physical, mental, and spiritual development of young people so that they may take a constructive place in society'; earlier than this, in 1883, the Boys' Brigade was founded 'for the advancement of Christ's Kingdom among boys and promotion of the habits of obedience, reverence, discipline, self-respect and all that leads towards a true Christian manliness'. There are many organizations for adults imbued with the same mildly exemplarist tone. The most interesting, perhaps, is the Samaritans, a nation-wide organization in Britain which operates a telephone service available to people who feel themselves to be in desperate need or even on the verge of committing suicide, and who want help or just a sympathetic ear.[22] This organization attracts as helpers – as 'Good Samaritans' – many people who think of themselves as Christians, and yet who feel marginal to the Church as an organiztion and who feel that much of the Church's teaching is marginal to them.

And finally there is the exemplarism which continues to exist in the culture of the unchurched working class. There is no need, I think, to add further to what was said above in connection with Richard Hoggart's acute observations.

Exemplarism, then, is the first distinct style of religiousness. No doubt there are those who would deny that it is religion at all, and certainly that it is Christian,[23] but that is a religious argument rather than a sociological one. If people who think of themselves as 'religious' or as 'Christians' hold these views, it is for sociologists to ensure that they do not measure religiousness in such a way as to exclude these people.

3 Conversionism

The second type of religiousness to be described is no less complex than the first, but unlike exemplarism it is unambiguously recognizable as both 'religious' and 'Christian'. Like exemplarism, it appeals in different ways to different social classes, and it can appear in many guises, but it is a clearly definable style of religiousness.

One of the problems of using ideal types is particularly obvious in describing this second style of religiousness, which I shall call *conversionism*, because there are many practising Christians who roughly correspond to the type. This is why it is so unambiguously recognizable as religious and Christian. Precisely because it is an ideal type which is being drawn, however, there is a danger that I may be thought to be exaggerating, or giving a somewhat one-sided account, or even parodying. Parody has no place in the construction of an ideal type, or it should not have; on the other hand an exaggerated and one-sided account is exactly what an ideal type should be, in order that it may bring out as clearly as possible the implicit character of the phenomenon being typified. The problem cannot be avoided but one can at least be prepared for it.

The compelling reality of Jesus Christ can be experienced in more ways than one. We have seen how the life of Jesus can be a powerful and compelling example of how life should be lived, and the words of Pontius Pilate, 'Behold the man', have often been interpreted by preachers in this way. There is another way, however, in which Jesus can appeal to people: he is still the focus, but he is the focus of a totally different type of religiousness.

Exemplarism, as we have seen, starts from the assumption that the world and human nature are basically good. Why there should be so much cruelty and suffering in the world is a perplexing problem, but exemplarism hopes that the problem would be solved if only we could become like Jesus of Nazareth, for then not only would we conquer the ills within and outside ourselves, but we would help the whole creation to move nearer and nearer to the Kingdom which Jesus said was at hand. But there are others who doubt whether human nature is intrinsically good, and doubt whether nature as a whole is benevolent. The second type of religious attitude, conversionism, gives an emphatically negative answer to both questions.

The tendency to fall short of the ideal we set for ourselves, which is the common experience of us all, is the most basic characteristic of human nature according to conversionism; it is like a great weight hung around our necks which pulls us down, try as we may to do better. No matter how hard we try to bring up our children to be gentle and loving, they too seem to be afflicted with the same mysterious malaise which constantly reasserts itself in generation after generation. The picture drawn by William Golding in *Lord of the Flies* is all too true. Nor is it human nature alone which is thus cursed, for the whole world is flawed. There are earthquakes and droughts, but even worse than that, the whole of nature is bloody and ugly, 'red in tooth and claw'. William Temple, calling this phenomenon 'the sin of the world', said that it

> pervades the universe. It accounts for the cruelty of the jungle
> where each animal follows its own appetite, unheeding and
> unable to heed any general good. It becomes conscious, and
> therefore tenfold more virulent, in man.[1]

To be aware of the sin of the world as a great burden which weighs us down is, *ipso facto*, to long for relief from the pain it inflicts. If one recognizes that there is this 'infection of nature', which extends to man who is 'of his own nature inclined to evil',[2] then one longs to be saved from this plight. It is in Jesus Christ that those who are saved from sin find the answer to this longing.

The most fundamental feature of conversionism is that it is based on a real and immediate experience, rather than on a hope or an aspiration: the experience of having been set free from the weight of sin, released from a burden, and alive in an entirely new way. Most of us have some familiarity with the conversion experience and indeed most of us have had friends or relations who have been converted, but too few people recognize the power of the experience or the complete transformation which it effects in the believer's life. If we are to understand it we must start from an imaginative reconstruction of what the world and human nature looks like to one who has been saved. One person wrote: 'I came to the Lord Jesus for salvation on 30th April 1955. Before that time I was continually seeking for satisfaction. I knew I was a sinner, but had no power to stop sinning.' (1133) The person who has received salvation, or been converted, recognizes the utter powerlessness and lostness of those who have not come to Christ. Nor is this an individual or subjective matter only. The world is lost and society is powerless. Another letter expresses the objective situation thus:

> The problems confronting men and women today are colossal; they are truly superhuman difficulties – they are beyond the power of nature, beyond the resources of man to cope with. . . . A supernatural gospel is our only hope, because we are incapable of solving our problems on our own. If the old-fashioned way is wrong and untrue, then I feel we are faced with hopeless despair. (1791)

Both subjectively and objectively, life is hopeless for the conversionist. Those who have finally found salvation often searched long for a satisfactory life, as this letter shows:

> Before my conversion life was just pointless and without any purpose. I searched for peace, for satisfaction, for a life with a real meaning and purpose. More than that I searched for security, for something or someone in whom I could put my trust, who in turn could offer me freedom from fear, the fear of death.
>
> As I have said I searched, but I could not find. I tried the world and *all* that it had to offer, but all was in vain. My search for true peace, satisfaction, security, led me into many vices from whose grip I could not free myself. At this stage I knew myself to be hopelessly bound by sin, I could not free myself from its hold on me, so I went on not because I *wanted* to, but because I *had* to. (1424)

We have seen how the life of Jesus can be an example for those who feel on their own in the world, and can provide a vital source of inspiration to soldier on in the hope that one may follow where Jesus has led. In stark contrast, those who feel themselves to be so totally infected by sin as to be totally incapacitated by it find that a mere example falls derisively short of what they need. Where exemplarists think they must face up to the harsh reality and recognize that they are on their own, somehow finding the courage to be, conversionists find the idea that human beings are on their own a horrifying one, a prospect which leaves them utterly without hope. What for the exemplarist is a hard fact to be faced is unfaceable for the conversionist: it could be only a recipe for despair. Such an idea is not just unbearable to the conversionist; it is also plainly wrong. There can be no question of Jesus being merely an example. What people need is to be saved, not encouraged, and it is only God who can save us. One person explains the error of thinking otherwise than in those terms:

> Take away the person of God, and man is left to be his own God. This is of course one of the chief glories of the atheist, to believe that he has a world in which man = God. In other words man is the arbiter and controller of the world, and man embodies the criterion of what good living, useful existence, really is. . . . [The effect is] to present man with the manifestly false opinion that God's image in Man is still unsullied, and man still has no need whatever of redemption. (1114)

This thoroughgoing image of human nature and the whole of creation as utterly corrupt is a basic ingredient of conversionism as a type of religiousness. If that were one's considered view, life would indeed be a most miserable affair, and one would long to be saved from the grip of so unhappy and wicked a world. The conversionist, however, always gives this frightening report of unregenerate life from the other side of the conversion experience, as one who has already been saved from it, and one wonders if it looked quite as black at the time as it does in retrospect.

In seeking to understand the undoubtedly true and real experiences of conversionism two points must be borne in mind. The first is that we all see the past from the standpoint of the present, and it is impossible for us to do otherwise. Exemplarism, with its emphasis on hope for the future, tends to see the present in the light of what might be, and that too is a common experience. The present has the special property of containing both past and future, being their product and their origin respectively. Eliot expressed it with the poet's precision in 'Burnt Norton':

> Time past and time future
> What might have been and what has been
> Point to one end, which is always present.

The quality of life as one knew it in the past is thus necessarily subject to reinterpretation from the perspective of the present, and the result of this reinterpretation is inevitably all the more dramatic if a conversion experience separates the past from the present. Even the experience of conversion itself can sometimes be recognized only with the benefit of hindsight, as I discovered in a piece of research some years ago. In the course of interviewing men who were about to enter colleges for training Anglican clergymen I asked the men whether they had had an experience of conversion. Of those who were going to an Evangelical college, where to have been converted was the norm, most, but not all, of the men said that they had; when asked the same question again after several months in college, however, they all said that they had been converted, and those who previously had not said so were able at this later interview to put dates to their conversion experiences, which were all prior to the first round of interviews.[3] So the horror in which the world is held by those who have been saved is more understandable when one bears in mind their present experience of having been saved from it.

The second point which needs to be noted is that, at least for some people, what is good and beautiful becomes all the more so not only by virtue of its own inherent qualities, but also in comparison with the foulness and ugliness which is evident elsewhere. Some people are not content to be told that they are in the right, but need to be told further how wholly in the wrong are their opponents. It is possible that conversionists achieve a lively sense of how beautiful it is to be saved, not only from their present sense of wonderful freedom, but also by painting a picture of life before conversion in lurid colours. The vigorous condemnation of unregenerate life serves to encourage converts to continue in their new way, and also helps to keep alive an urgent sense of the world's need for conversion. Comparatively minor lapses and indiscretions, therefore, and perhaps things which are 'naughty but nice', may be aspects of a conversionist's earlier life which, after conversion, take on the appearance of full-blown vices.

Those two points made, it nevertheless remains a part of the conversionist's experience that life does change with conversion, and change dramatically. Perhaps an acute sense of despair is not necessary for a person to come to conversion, but there must be some sense of dis-ease, some sensed need, or at least an unease which is recognized only immediately prior to the conversion experience. Then after conversion, and in the light of the experience of having received salvation, a person's former life takes on a new appearance and is recognized as having been the horrific mess it was, although this may be an *ex post facto* recognition. But whether it is extreme despair or just a general malaise, the crucial point for the conversionist is when it is resolved as a result of accepting Christ into one's life: one accepts a wholly new set of ideas about oneself, about one's life, and about the world. This is the moment of truth, the turning point, the point of no return; this is when the whole universe assumes a new meaning, and it is the result of the individual's accepting, as a massively traumatic fact, that he or she cannot 'go it alone'. Therefore he or she dies; from this point on the old person is dead, is born again as a new person, and lives now the life of Christ. Whereas formerly nothing was possible, now all things are possible, and this is so only by virtue of having been saved. As one letter put it:

> Only Christ can live the Christian life, and He wants to live out His life and purpose through us as His earthen vessels, and He cannot begin to do that until we are converted, born again of His Spirit, for 'the natural man received not the things of the Spirit of God . . . neither can he know them, because they are spiritually discerned.' Of our human nature God says, 'We are all as an unclean thing, and even our righteousnesses are as filthy rags.' The Bible tells us that only that which is born again of Christ's spirit, that which is clothed in His righteousness, can enter Heaven, (1656)

It is the experience of having been born again that truly matters, and it is so real and vivid an experience that all else pales into insignificance. Another letter expresses it thus:

> 'Except a man be born again he cannot see the Kingdom of God'; my own experience of this being, as so often in men's experience, an initial and unerasable conviction, experience and assurance of God's combined forgiveness and presence, through coming as a sinner, under the Promises of God (which cannot fail, ever) to my only Master, Saviour, and crucified sin-bearer. (1114)

We must be clear that this is religious conviction at its very strongest: it is not an opinion, or a religious preference, but a certainty about the way the world is, and the conviction is reckoned to be of universal validity, for as the last letter quoted goes on:

> no man or woman has ever even begun to experience the joys of life, of right relationships at their deepest level, the indescribable yet wonderful and true fact of real and constant and daily pece with God, who has not first received forgiveness of sins. (1114)

Words fail the correspondent, who cannot find a way of

expressing adequately what is so overwhelmingly real to him.

The experience of 'having been saved from sin' is the heart of conversionism as a style of religiousness. And one must be precise about what the experience is which matters: it is not the experience of *being* converted, but the experience of *having been* converted. Some people are 'converted', in the sense of going forward in a religious service to accept Christ as their saviour, more than once, and indeed some do it many times in their lives, but that is not the experience which is central to conversionism. The characteristic experience is the continuous one of having started life afresh. So the experience which is typical of conversionism is not to be confused with the range of experiences examined by students of 'religious experience',[4] although initiation into conversionism as a style of religiousness is usually marked by the experience of *being* converted. We may note, incidentally, the conclusion of E.M. Starbuck on the permanence of the effects of a conversion experience, as quoted by William James, which is that it brings,

> a changed attitude towards life, which is fairly constant and permanent, although the feelings fluctuate. . . . In other words, the persons who have passed through conversion, *having once taken a stand for the religious life*, tend to feel themselves identified with it, no matter how much their religious enthusiasm declines.[5]

In other words, the singular experience of conversion marks a beginning: 'having once taken a stand for the religious life'. The experience to which I am drawing attention here is what follows, and is characteristic of those who 'feel themselves identified' with a style of religiousness in which the continuing experience of *having been* converted is of central importance.

The terminology employed by various religious groups in which this style of religiousness is prominent is diverse. I take 'being converted', 'coming to Christ', 'saved from sin', 'born again', and 'baptised in the Spirit', as well as expressions which are short biblical quotations such as, 'washed in the blood of the lamb', to be equivalents. Each denotes a new beginning, and it is the experience of having made that new beginning which is important for conversionism as a style of religiousness.[6]

If having been saved is what is crucial in being a Christian, the Church, which numbers very many who have not had this experience, is almost as much of a problem to conversionists as it is to exemplarists. In practice, it is simply an embarrassment, for in the eyes of those who have been saved from sin, the Church proper includes only those who are twice-born. In a way, those who have not been re-born are worse than confessed unbelievers, for they blur the vital distinction between those who have received the Spirit and those who have not. This is particularly obvious when a person is born again after many years as a church-goer, as we see in the following letter:

> As I write these lines the time is 10.25 on the eve of my 59th birthday. Forty of that a Church of England man: only a hypocrite. But the last years I gave myself to God, my life changed. Now I want to work for my Saviour, praise his name. (612)

This vital experience can follow years of apparently Christian living and of seemingly serious commitment, as another letter makes amply clear:

> I am a woman in middle age; I was brought up in a happy so-called Christian family: we were all church workers, I taught in the Sunday school; and I married a parson (he died in 1941). I never really doubted the existence of God and what I believed to be the Christian faith. By the mercy and grace of God, six years ago I was born again. I faced the Truth in a personal confrontation with the Living Lord, Who said, 'I *am* the TRUTH'. Gradually, as more and more has been revealed, my innermost being has come to know the REALITY of
> 'I am the WAY, the TRUTH, and the LIFE.'
> I know Him as my *personal* Saviour and Lord, know that I am cleansed by His Blood and born again of His Spirit, so that I can say with Paul, 'I am crucified with Christ: nevertheless I live; yet not I, but Christ lives in me.' (1656)

For conversionists, the Church is the community of those who have been born again. Membership of the Church of England, or even of the Roman Catholic Church, can be of less significance to the twice-born than is the sense of belonging to the company of those who have experienced re-birth, and so we find that conversionists will short-circuit the laborious efforts of the ecumenical movement and join together in forms of worship which express their shared experience.

Despite its impatience with the Church, conversionism is characterized by a high doctrine of the Church. Indeed, it is this high doctrine which gives rise to its impatience with the formal organization which calls itself the Church. Conventionally, theologians restrict the expression 'high doctrine of the Church' to the view that it is Christ's continuing presence on earth and that as such it rightly demands the obedience of Christians. It is the view expressed by Newman in a verse in *The Dream of Gerontius*:

> And I hold in veneration,
> For the love of Him alone,
> Holy Church, as His creation,
> And her teachings, as His own.

Sociologically, however, it is helpful to extend the meaning of the term and to identify the typically protestant view of the Church as a second kind of high doctrine,[7] in order to free the expression 'low doctrine of the Church' to characterize those types of religiousness which reject external authority.[8] Exemplarism has a low doctrine of the Church because of its emphasis on the individual, and in subsequent chapters we shall consider other styles of religiousness which, though for different reasons, also have a low doctrine. Conversionism has a high doctrine in the sense that the Church, i.e. the community of believers, is indispensable to it. Only in the Church can conversionists find *koinonia,* fellowship, with others who are living the new life. We shall see shortly that this is an integral part of conversionism, but at this point it needs only to be noted that conversionism's hostility to – or at least tension with – the Churches does not imply that it holds the Church in anything less than the highest esteem.

The certainty which is born of the experience of having been converted is remarkable, and to believers it is glorious and awe-inspiring; but, inevitably, it leads to a position where others must be judged. One letter said plainly:

> Although you are a Bishop and I am only a twenty-one year old girl I make no apologies for saying that you do not know the Lord Jesus Christ as your Saviour, and therefore you are still a child of the Devil as I once was. (1133)

How should one characterize belief of this kind? How can one define the cognitive style which is proper to conversionism? The word 'belief' is hardly appropriate since it fails to convey the certainty known to conversionists as a result of their experience of having been saved. One possibility is the word 'faith'. It has the advantage that it connects with the theological dichotomy of faith and works, and conversionism certainly sees salvation as being through faith, not works. It has the further advantage of connecting with popular usage. 'I wish I had your faith' commonly means that one wishes one had the certainty the other person obviously enjoys; and the phrase, 'blind faith', too, is in common use, although it is employed as a derogatory expression more often, perhaps, than as a term of envy or approval. The disadvantages outweigh the advantages, however, both because the word 'faith' is so fraught with theological arguments, and also, and more importantly, because it fails to convey the sense of certainty. The expression I prefer is 'assurance'. That it is a common term in the devotional language of conversionism is to its advantage, and we capture the cognitive style best if we read the phrase 'I believe' as meaning, 'I am assured'. Putting the verb in the passive mood is important, too, for all the familiar phrases of conversionism are in the passive rather than the active: being born again, saved, converted, baptised in the spirit.[9] What is conveyed is that something has *happened to* the believer who has been the passive victim of an activity from without, and this is exactly what the language is meant to convey, for it is the way in which the event is experienced. The language expresses the idea that human beings are mere nothings; that the best they can do is no better than 'filthy rags'; that they are tools wielded by invisible hands. The language not only embodies this idea, it glorifies it and presents it as good, on the sole condition that it is in the hands of God that people are wielded as tools.[10]

The message is this: human beings are worthless, corrupt and vicious; they are powerless and under the control of malign forces; their only hope is to become the willing slaves of God. In accepting men and women as his slaves, God does them an infinite favour since they are so totally depraved and worthless; in slavery to God, men and women will find infinite happiness and contentment, neither of which is theirs by nature, and which they find thanks only to the unbounded generosity of God in sacrificing his son as a substitute for sinful humanity. The gospel is the good news of this possibility, and the gospel story is the account of how God has made salvation possible for us.

This message of salvation is either accepted or rejected. There is no middle ground. If the offer of salvation is accepted, one must accept it as a little child, asking of one's Heavenly Father, and the result will be a life spent in the continuous presence of God. In outward appearance this new life may be no different, and it may not be without problems, but the transformed life is worthwhile beyond any shadow of doubt. The decision is taken only once, but its effect is permanent so that it is possible to say 'I now walk with Him daily.' (650) 'Walk with God' becomes a synonym for life, for the whole of it is spent with God at one's side. If there are problems in feeling this constant presence it is the result of failings somewhere, either in the believer or in the insidious influence of the world, for it should not be so. Most problems, as one letter put it, are:

fostered by the low level of example and of social conventions

> accepted in high places in Christendom; but, praise God, the humblest Christian can through God's grace in some matters be wiser than those in the Church set over him. (1114)

Prayer takes its place at this point. For conversionism it is not something set apart but the constant conversation with the invisible friend and master; and public worship provides the occasions when servants of the Lord come together to celebrate their master and their brotherhood in his service. The prayer life of the conversionist is like that of the monk or nun in many respects, for every effort is made to think about God in every situation and without interruption, much as a Religious might seek to be in a perpetual state of 'recollection'. There are differences, of course, for when this religious ideal is (in Weber's words) carried out of monastic cells into everyday life it meets a thousand problems and decisions which the regime of the convent solves in advance. So the conversionist takes every situation 'to the Lord in prayer', whether it be a business decision, the question of where to go on holiday, or whether to have sexual intercourse: every matter is referred to God in the certain knowledge that he will give clear guidance. The similarity of conversionism to the Religious life is not surprising. Given the fact of the converionist's 'calling' to a new life, that life is bound to parallel in certain respects the special life to which the Religious feels called, and, significantly, they share the experience of *having been called*.

As I observed earlier, the Church, the fellowship of other disciples, is absolutely essential for those who have been saved from sin. At first sight there seems to be a paradox here: on the one hand conversionism is the most individualistic of religious attitudes because the personal experience of having been converted is central, but on the other hand it depends for its very existence upon the group of believers, and an isolated conversionist is almost a contradiction in terms. If the religion of the conversionist hinges on individual, personal, immediate experience, why is the Church of such importance? The answer, I suggest, is that a 'new life' begun in one's adult years is essentially precarious, and depends for its survival upon the support of the community of others who share the new life which the conversionist knows. This point requires some elaboration, but there is one feature of the 'individual experience' which must be noted first.

Those who have been converted, who have been saved from sin, do not first have the experience of being converted and then, afterwards, meet with others who have had the same experience.[11] We must remember that the characteristic experience of conversionism is not *being* converted, but *having been* converted. The call to a new life in Christ is a calling from Christ, to be sure, but Christ's call is proclaimed by the Church. It is the group of those who know themselves to have been converted, or a representative of the group, who tells the potential convert of the possibility of a new life in Christ. The invitation to accept Christ as one's personal saviour, therefore, is at the same time an invitation to join the group of those who already know him to be their saviour. The 'personal relationship with God' is an intimacy, but it is shared with the group of intimates.

So the individual decision for Christ is social as well as individual. Joining the company of those who know they have been converted is indissolubly linked to the experience of oneself coming to the knowledge that one has been converted.

The Church is important to conversionism because the Church is the group of the converted, and those whose religiousness is dominated by the experience of having been converted must for ever draw and re-draw the dividing line between themselves and the rest, between the saved and the damned. The boundary of a sect is clear, but the boundary which surrounds conversionists is not, and therefore its existence needs to be marked, in order that the experience of 'having been converted' should remain fresh and alive.

Indeed, two boundaries define the world of conversionism. The first is the boundary which cuts across the life of every conversionist, dividing the person's biography into two: before crossing the boundary one was a miserable sinner, lost in despair; having crossed it one has been born anew in the life of Christ. The second boundary divides the world into two: those who have been saved and those who have not. In order that conversionists' identities should remain secure, both boundaries must be continually marked. The first is marked by telling and re-telling the story of one's life, of how it truly began only when one accepted the Lord Jesus, and how wretched life had been before that day. The second boundary is marked chiefly by bringing others to conversion and welcoming them into the community of the twice-born. These two boundaries define the Church, the fellowship of those who know that they have been saved.

We saw that the problem of evil does not really exist as a problem for exemplarism. Faced with pain and suffering, the exemplarist takes it as a challenge and defies it to do its worst. If conversionism is so different a style of religiousness, how does it react when faced with evil? Typically, the person who has been saved from sin says that it is of no importance. Compared with the assurance of having been saved, it is trivial. Human suffering is always a source of perplexity, but the pain, which does not go away because one has turned to Christ, is not allowed to constitute a problem for conversionism. Instead, like Christ who bore suffering 'for the joy that was set before him', one thinks only of one's salvation, and rivetting one's attention on Christ's promises one treats pain as a test one knows that one will pass. If you ask conversionists why a good God should allow so much misery in the world he has made, you will find that they simply do not see the problem. All they know is the joy of salvation. And since there is no problem, there is no answer. Conversionism, therefore, has no theodicy.

We have already, in passing, seen some of the beliefs about God which are associated with this type of religiousness, and it will be clear that they are orthodoxly trinitarian. Without a moment's hesitation, conversionism will say, as one letter does:

> I know God as my Father. I know that the second Person of the Godhead, my precious Beloved Lord and Master died to redeem me, and that the Lovely Holy Spirit abides in me. (1133)

Conversionists do not need to believe, for they know. As another letter expressed it:

> It would be absurd, surely, to say to any Christian, 'Your God is not a Person, a transcendent Person'; as much tell him, as far as his own experience is concerned, 'Your parents are not people'! (1114)

My contention is that this certain knowledge which is based on personal and immediate experience is entirely real for the conversionist, but that the experience is wholly one of having been saved. Private prayer, public worship, and converting others are all activities which revitalize the experience, and serve to keep it alive as a constantly remembered fact. The certain knowledge which is ascribed to theological doctrines about God, Jesus, the Holy Spirit, the atonement, and so on, enables us to recognize these beliefs as an elaborate set of shibboleths. When a conversionist says, 'I know that the Lovely Holy Spirit abides in me', she is actually reiterating the certainty with which she knows that she has been saved, rather than saying that this is another and separate matter about which she has equally certain knowledge. For the conversionist, subscribing to an orthodox creed is a way of asserting the reality of the central experience through the medium of a complex set of symbols. This is not to deny the importance of the symbols or to doubt their potency.

One recognizes the way in which a flag, for example, though it is only a sign, may have significance in its own right for the man who fights under it. As Durkheim wrote:

> The soldier who dies for his flag, dies for his country; but as a matter of fact in his own consciousness, it is the flag that has the first place. It sometimes happens that this even directly determines action. Whether one isolated standard remains in the hands of the enemy or not does not determine the fate of the country, yet the soldier allows himself to be killed to regain it. He loses sight of the fact that the flag is only a sign, and that it has no value in itself, but only brings to mind the reality it represents; it is treated as if it were this reality itself.[12]

My argument is a parallel one: when conversionists profess absolutely certain knowledge of the truth of the Christian creed, they are giving expression to their certain knowledge of the experience of having been saved from sin, but in their own consciousness they believe themselves to be convinced of the truth of the entire creed in all its particulars.

Conversionism is comprised, then, of the twin propositions that human beings need to be saved from sin, and that the individual knows himself or herself to have been so saved. Every aspect of this type of religiousness rests on these twin propositions, and nothing can have any validity unless it is derived from them. The human experience of love, for example, might be thought to be something whose goodness is self-authenticating, but this cannot be granted by conversionists, who argue that love derives from the love of God, which in its turn is possible only for the convert. A letter put it simply and straightforwardly: 'Love considered independently of conversion is a mistake, because the love of God is given to us through conversion, through the Holy Spirit's indwelling.' (1114) In other words, conversionism is a total world-view, resting on the experience of having been saved. It is not unlike other total world-views, for we find that the psychoanalyst and the revolutionary, in common with the conversionist, will say in less guarded moments that one cannot understand, much less attain any true experience of music, politics, literature, economics, justice, art, war or love, except from the perspective which it provides, be it analysis, the dawning of the revolution, or conversion. One might make a case for the revolutionary since, grounded in the hope of a society which will be free from oppression, it asserts only that all our present knowledge must be provisional, but the case for conversionism cannot be argued, and does not ask to be argued. Its appeal is to experience. Conversionism is assured that to be converted and saved from sin is to have new life in Christ; that, and that alone, gives men and women the ability to see the world as it really is. The rest of humanity, atheists, communists, Jews, heathen, and once-born Christians alike, are still fallen creatures, trapped in their sinfulness.

The moral code which is accepted by conversionism, like its code of theological doctrine, is absolute and God-given. 'Love' can be no guide, as we have seen, for happiness too is the prerogative of the saved. So a moral law is necessary because of the sinfulness of humankind in general. As one letter said:

> God *has* given *laws* for life, and if these are disregarded a
> society becomes steadily more and more dissolute, corrupt,
> and spineless. The Ten Commandments remain in essence a
> statement of God's laws. Immorality is the result in every
> society (not excluding many so-called Christian societies)
> where God's laws are treated as a basis for discussion instead
> of being realised as a God-ordained basis for human
> relationships. (1114)

Again, the argument rests on the fundamental contention that human beings need to be saved from the sinfulness which is their inherent nature.

The world holds no charms for the conversionist. Secular, unredeemed culture at its most innocent threatens to distract one's gaze from salvation, and may delude one into believing that it has some intrinsic value, whereas the truth is that nothing has escaped the taint of sin and therefore nothing can be of value in itself. Everything, however, may be brought into the service of the new creation, so long as it has been redeemed. As George Herbert's hymn put it:

> All may of thee partake;
> Nothing can be so mean,
> Which with this tincture, 'for thy sake',
> Will not grow bright and clean.

Thus an ordinary job of work meets with the approval of conversionism, as does the rearing of a family.[13] Not all jobs are equally acceptable, however, and certain intellectual pursuits are fraught with danger. The arts and humanities in particular are viewed with suspicion, for they tend to strive for a human vision which can rival the Christian vision. Just as love is good only 'through the Holy Spirit's indwelling', so 'good music', and 'good theatre' are music and theatre which serve the Lord. Conversionism views independent canons of artistic judgment to be hazardous in the extreme.[14] The sciences, on the other hand, are comparatively safe since they concern a mechanical understanding of the way the world works rather than an understanding of why anything should be.[15] That is why this type of religiousness appeals to doctors, scientists, men of war and men of commerce, rather than artists or men of letters.

Political activities are seen by conversionists as being strictly means to short-term ends, for if the world is to be brought to God it can be only as the result of individual men and women being saved, one by one. Politics may hope to remove some barriers, but in itself it cannot advance the Kingdom of God by a single inch, and there is the constant danger that people may substitute political concerns for a single-minded care for the salvation of individuals. Therefore conversionism is chary of politics. The only changes which it regards as worth making are those which directly facilitate the conversion of men and women, and even the amelioration of suffering for which Evangelicalism was renowned in nineteenth-century England was justified in such terms, and seen as a manifest fruit of the Spirit at work among the philanthropic converts.

The consequences of this a-political stance have been strangely different in various places and at various times, and the divergence has never been more apparent than it is today among Pentecostalists in different parts of the world. No contrast could be more striking than that between, for example, the member of an independent black pentecostal Church in a South African township, and a white charismatic bishop in the same country, though the religiousness of each is dominated by conversionism. The black's religion may be the only way in which he can express his rejection of the political order imposed on him, and indeed may be a proto-political activity. The bishop's position is an altogether different one, for when the a-political option is chosen by someone who is not actively oppressed and forcibly excluded from power, that option in reality is highly political.

Conversionism represents the most important sectarian element constantly to have re-vitalized Christianity, and its influence, demanding fresh and total commitment to the religious enterprise, has often prevented the Church from becoming cold and staid and tired. That has not been its only role, however. Just as often it has made the Christian religion into what Marx accurately described as the opium of the people: a highly addictive drug which soothes the pain but does nothing to effect a cure. As it occurs today in the western world (as opposed to the socialist countries and 'developing' societies), conversionism is as much a response to secular culture as is exemplarism. The Christian message is not adapted to the contemporary world, it is true, but it is popular because of prevailing social conditions. The 'born-again Christians' who are becoming more numerous and more conspicuous have embraced a type of religiousness which saves them from what they believe to be a nasty world. And that belief, together with their other beliefs, deserves serious attention. Conversionism does nothing to alter the world, however, and indeed believes that nothing can be done except by individuals coming to personal salvation: thereafter they remain in the world, but are not of the world.

For our present purpose, the principal importance of conversionism is methodological rather than substantive, despite its considerable substantive interest. Conversionism is important because, too easily, it is seen as being 'ordinary' religion, but in a very intense way. My argument is that it is but one way of being religious, and that it must be recognized as one amongst others. On the standard sociological survey of religion the conversionist will come out as being 'very religious'. That is fair, but only so long as he or she is seen as 'very religious' in a particular way. The way, the conversionist way, is identifiable by three principal characteristics: the experience of having been saved, or converted, or born again, is strongly affirmed; human beings are believed to be naturally wicked; and non-religious culture is held to be of little significance. The strongly asserted belief in a range of conventional doctrines should not be allowed to disguise the importance of these three distinguishing characteristics.

4   Theism

In a review of John Robinson's work, C.S. Lewis wrote:

> If I were briefed to defend his position I should say, 'The image of Earth-Mother gets in something which that of the Sky-Father leaves out. Religions of the Earth-Mother have hitherto been spiritually inferior to those of the Sky-Father, but, perhaps, it is now time to readmit some of their elements.' I shouldn't believe it very strongly, but some sort of case could be made out.[1]

The remark may or may not be fair in the context, but the two general points made by Lewis are sound, i.e., that in the view of many people natural religion has something to commend it, and that it has been discouraged by traditional Christianity. *Theism* is the name I shall give here to the type of religious attitude which focuses on God and his creation. It has something in common with the several doctrines which were called Deism and were current in the late seventeenth and eighteenth centuries; it is different both because it is a popular form of religiousness rather than a philosophical system, and also because it has closer affinities with the ideas of the Old Testament than was ever true of Deism.

Most people would define religion as belief in God, but we have seen two kinds of religious attitude for which that would be a misleading description; here we encounter a form of religiousness which conforms to it well enough. Theism acknowledges that there must be a creator, and that this creator is benevolent. God is the centre; he makes sense of the world as it appears to us and of our experience of it; he lends significance to what, without him, would have to be regarded as arbitrary; above all he enables us to see order and purpose in both the physical and moral universe.

It is not only ordinary simple people who think of religion as belief in a benevolent creator God; many of those who have studied religion scientifically and who have offered theories to explain it have shared this view. Freud, Feuerbach and Müller, to name just three, were explaining something approximating to what I have called theism when they gave their accounts of religion, though the Church they had in mind was the oppressive institution it has commonly been in history. This has been a legitimate approach since theism is the bed-rock of all western styles of religion. Other types of religious attitude, such as the ones described elsewhere in this volume, are developments from it, or extensions or modifications of it. It would be otherwise if our perspective were from the East rather than from the West, and it is worth remarking that what purport to be general theories of religion propounded in the West, turn out, on closer examination, to be theories of western religion.[2] The perspective employed here, however, and the types of religiousness described, are western. I am making no attempt to universalize.

When theists look at the world they judge it to be very good. As a religious attitude, theism is grounded in a sense of wonder and awe in the face of the beauty and order of nature, and it cannot accept that the world is thus as the result of chance or impersonal forces, for only an infinitely careful plan could possibly have made the world as it is. As the writer of one letter put it: 'I am a believer in God mainly for the simple reason that I believe "The heavens declare the glory of God and the firmament showeth his handiwork." ' (2782)

Of the two basic strands in western theology, this represents the strand which sees God in his creation and is called natural religion. In the other strand, called revealed religion, God reveals himself directly and has personal relations both with individuals and with nations. In practice, the more that attention has been paid to God's immediate revelation of himself and of his will, the less has it been focused on the creation as an expression of the creator God. Revealed religion always builds on the foundation of natural religion, but, superseding it, claims a higher and more immediate authority. Natural religion does not die, however, and when revealed religion hesitates, loses confidence, or begins to doubt its overriding authority, natural religion is ever ready to reassert its insights as the bed-rock of all religion. The image of gender argues that the Sky-Father is domineering and unanswerable, exercising an authority which is as undependable as it is imperious, while the Earth-Mother is all-embracing and undemanding, totally dependable though she be ignored, flouted or abused, and her arms are always there waiting to receive again the creature who falls back into them. The Earth-Mother provides the security which enables self-confidence to grow. The Sky-Father excites ambition and inspires great deeds. But it is the Earth-Mother who gives comfort in the event of a failure which the Sky-Father may be expected to judge, condemn, and punish. Weber analysed the tension in religious organizations between a creative element, prophetic or charismatic in character, and a countervailing element which tends to make a priest out of every prophet and to stabilize each exciting innovation as a permanent tradition. Essentially the same tension has been expressed more recently by Victor Turner in terms of *communitas* and *societas*, anti-structure and structure.[3] It is clear that such analyses gain in generality only by ignoring details which are important to particular cultures, and a study of the Judaeo-Christian tradition must take account not only of the universal tension between tradition and innovation but also the particular struggle between the Earth-Mother and the Sky-Father which has taken place within it.

Wonder and awe, once it has been evoked or learned, may be expressed in many ways. Theism, I suggest, is the way which is most basic to western culture. In this religious attitude the wonder and the awe are focused on the person of God, so that what confronts the believer is no longer simply a wonderful and awesome world, but a God who is solely responsible for all that evokes these responses. God becomes synonymous with all that is wonderful or awesome. By the same token, the position of the human being is no more than that of the creature in the face of its creator. In a polytheistic or magical world, populated by spirits or gods who are individually responsible for waterfalls, thunderstorms, love affairs, and so on, people have a multitude of forces to contend with, but they may pit their wits against them almost as equals. They may bribe them one by one, or even try to set them at odds with one another. Confronted with the One Creator God one can pretend to no equality at all. One is reduced to saying with the psalmist:

> O Lord our Governor, how excellent is thy name in all the world:
> Thou that hast set thy glory above the heavens!
> For I will consider thy heavens, even the works of thy fingers:
> The moon and the stars which thou hast ordained.
> What is man that thou art mindful of him:

> And the son of man that thou visitest him?

Here and throughout the psalms God is present not just as the Earth-Mother, but as the Sky-Father as well. He visits 'the children of men' and has dealings with them; he is encountered directly as well as being immanent in his handiwork. Theism, however, is the religious attitude of those who know God predominantly through his creation. It is not a religion solely of the Earth-Mother, but nor is it the religion of Abraham and Moses, who spoke to God 'face to face, as a man speaketh to his friend'. It is a religion whose adherents, while they know that others have encountered God directly, are themselves over-whelmingly aware of God indirectly, through the whole of creation.

Wonder and awe are the experiences in which theism is rooted, but these experiences may be predominantly either a matter of feeling or a matter of thinking. The emotional experience of God can range from a simple feeling of well-being to an ecstatic state accompanied by visions. For some, the lines of Thomas Traherne will ring true:

> Can you take too much joy in your Father's work? He is
> himself in everything. Some things are little on the outside and
> rough and common. But I remember the time when the dust
> of the streets was as precious as gold to my infant eye, and
> now it is more precious to the eye of reason.

While for others, Wordsworth may be nearer to the mark:

> Hence in a season of calm weather
> Though inland far we be,
> Our souls have sight of that immortal sea
> Which brought us hither,
> And see the children sport upon the shore,
> And hear the mighty waters rolling evermore.

For yet others it may be predominantly cognitive, springing from reflection on empirical experience, as in this letter:

> I've sometimes had an atheistic mood, but it soon goes when I
> think of the millions of stars, reproduction in plant and animal
> life and everyday, but complex nature. In fact, I look on God
> as Mother nature herself, and *I* feel religious walking through
> a field, when other people feel it kneeling in a Church. (2204)

God is always at the centre.

Theism is a religious attitude which is convinced that there is more to the everyday world we experience than meets the eye. It insists that there is another realm of reality, but that this other sphere is not discontinuous with the world of the senses: on the contrary it is an added dimension. The eternal does not peep round the corners of the natural or fill gaps in our understanding of it; it does not take over when men and women reach the limits of their physical endurance, or when they are confronted with moral problems which defeat their natural wisdom and ingenuity. The God of theism is not a God of the gaps in the natural world, nor a God beyond its limits. He is a God whose presence shines in and through the natural world, giving a new significance to nature and forcing the believer to view the world as what it seems to be, and, simultaneously, as more than it seems to be, for everything comes to be seen *sub specie aeternitatis*. Having glimpsed this vision of God it is possible to say, in the words of another letter:

> in some unexplained way it has opened my eyes, because everything has become 'more so' if you understand what I mean. [And so] I enjoy things more because trivial things that seemed terribly important and very often worrying return to their proper place, so that everything is better, because flowers smell more lovely and look more beautiful, a concert is more glorious, or a painting more enjoyable to look at. Even a day at the sea (probably wet!) with one's family more fun.(40)

God himself, it should be noticed, does not appear. He is known only by inference, and yet this wholly indirect encounter carries complete conviction. As the writer of another letter said:

> I believe that people should face up to the fact that they are endowed by God with the capacity to know God directly – what may be called the numinous experience. This experience may not come in conventional prayer but in the Wind and the Light of the mountains, the sacraments of nature. Christ's disciples were out-of-door men, mostly fishermen I believe, and the shepherds in the fields were the ones to hear and see the angels at the announcement of his birth. Even the three Wise Men were looking at the stars out in the open. (758)

Not surprisingly, with such a strong sense of the presence and the power of God, this type of religiousness accords to Jesus a place of only subsidiary importance. The fact that he was an historical figure is not questioned; nor is it doubted that his ethical teachings were the highest ideal to which human beings can aspire and that what Jesus said of the Father as caring for his creation is of supreme importance. No matter how important a teacher Jesus may have been, however, and notwithstanding his example of how we should stand in relation to God, it cannot accept that he is God. Exemplarism, as we have seen, tends to treat God as redundant; in theism the reverse is true. As one letter put it:

> I cannot see how it is necessary to postulate a Christ who is necessary to save mankind. After all, if we have an omnipotent and omnipresent God, surely another Saviour becomes unnecessary. In fact this notion is quite fantastic to my way of thinking. (2782)

The divinity of Jesus is not only redundant but it positively detracts from a proper attitude to God. According to theism, it is a systematic distortion of the teaching of Jesus, for, starting with St Paul, the Church has consistently obfuscated the truth about God by teaching that Jesus was in some way God himself; and it has further added to the confusion by talking about the Holy Spirit as in some sense distinguishable from the Creator God. Theism is a monotheistic religious attitude, and it rejects the doctrine of the trinity as an image of God.

By a strange irony, theism rejects the divine Jesus for the same reason that exemplarism rejects God. Each sees the additional doctrine as a gratuitous extra which detracts from the stature of human nature, for theism, like exemplarism, has a high doctrine of human nature. There is need of the divine Jesus if we are essentially wicked, but this is a view which theism rejects; instead it sees us as having been made in the image of God. I am not a fallen creature who needs to be rescued, according to theism, and in so far as the Christian religion seeks to persuade me that I am, it is distorting the truth.

If the set of beliefs I have called theism finds a recurrent failing in humanity, it is that we are too much concerned with ourselves and not enough with God, and the result is that we fail to accept our natural position as creatures. We need to abandon ourselves to the will of God. One of the letters expressed human destiny thus:

> To become as a child before God is a step higher for us than the farthest of our limits as human beings. To desire only to rest as a baby in the arms of God, instinctively knowing that we cannot understand and yet knowing that somehow he will fulfil our every need is the birth of faith. (1867)

The same idea can be expressed as a statement about human nature, rather than about human needs:

> I really cannot think that I am other than a part of this mighty

universe, brought by it into being, and sustained and used by it in its purposes and life, however inscrutable it all is to me . . . Of course man has *not* learned to cope without God. Man's creatureliness is the chief thing about him. Man's origin, being, and destiny are in God. All human history witnesses against man's self-sufficiency and expresses his weakness and incompleteness.(4)

Men and women are frail and vulnerable and in need of God, but this is a far cry from being wicked sinners. What impresses the theist is the mightiness and grandeur of God on the one hand, and the tininess and insignificance of men and women in comparison with him on the other hand. If we have a besetting sin it is that we lack trust in God.

This type of religious attitude has an equivocal attitude to the Church. At first sight it may appear that so personal and immediate a type of religion would feel no need of organization, but this is not so. The perception of an eternal dimension to everyday life needs to be expressed and celebrated in ritual form. The awareness of God may be an individual matter, but it asks to be shared and demands that it be acknowledged in some public form. This makes the failure of the Church to provide a proper setting for such a celebration a major concern for theism. The greatness and majesty of God are so obvious and so spectacular that they cry out for the response of recognition. This, theism assumes, is what the Church is for. It should express our awareness of God with the reverent enthusiasm and excited urgency of Jesus. In practice, however, the theist finds that what goes on in church is boring and bored, in every way the opposite of what it should be. A church may even be found to be the one place in the world where God is inaccessible. In nature, in art, and even in the grime of the city streets, God is present, and the eternal dimension to life is unavoidably obvious. In church, however, where these hints and glimpses should be made explicit, theism often finds only morbid introspection and obsessive sentimentality, complicated mythological stories which obscure God, and a group of people with an apparent taste for third-rate aesthetics. As a result, it is a normal characteristic of theism to eschew the Church, albeit with regret. Its religious insights are so adulterated in church that they are suffocated and die; its religious longings and its *mal du clocher* for the eternal are clothed by the institutional Church with so much seemingly irrelevant paraphernalia that they find there no adequate expression. Of course there are individual theists who survive within the Churches, but they do so by blithely ignoring most of what goes on in church, and by managing to impose their own meanings and interpretations on the services. Some theists may search out particular churches they find congenial because of the dignity of the services; some may go to services only in the quiet of the early morning, when there are few people and no hymns or sermons to distract them. Sometimes they are made to feel thoroughly guilty for not finding an authentic expression of their religious intuitions in the doctrines and practices of the Church. Typically, however – and it is the type which is being described here – theism is unchurched: the fellowship it finds in the Church is so busy and enthusiastic about its own affairs that there is never a moment for the sunset-touch.

This kind of religiousness has a very positive view of the world, seeing a transcendent significance in life without for a moment denigrating it as a purely natural experience. It is so concerned with accepting and being accepted that it knows little or no tension between what is, and what ought to be. Consequently, it is a highly conservative view of life, insisting that every cloud has a silver lining, that there is no wind so ill that it blows nobody any good, etc., etc. It is capable of giving peace of soul to the individual believer, but at the expense of any capacity to make peace of soul more readily attainable for the human race as a whole. The predominance of the Earth-Mother religion in theism makes it seek meaning in what is, and inhibits it from striving to recreate the world so that it may embody more perfectly the meaning which it has grasped. In this sense it is the opposite of exemplarism, though both see human nature and the world as essentially good.

The incipiently conservative nature of theism is brought out clearly when we consider its attitude to evil and suffering, since this obviously represents a very special problem for a type of religiousness which worships the God who made all things bright and beautiful. It must somehow find a way of coming to terms with things which are ugly and bad. The problem can be stated easily enough. In the words of one letter: 'I'm still thinking about the mystery of suffering. Surely it is one of the greatest problems of life. If the good things come from God, then the bad things also. . . .' (2222) Another letter put it thus:

> The real difficulty is the question how, if God is governing the world, it goes so badly. 'Truth for ever on the scaffold, wrong for ever on the throne . . . and God within the shadows keeping watch. . . .' O dear, can't he do more than that? (102)

This poses the question in its classical western form. God is good; God is almighty; and yet there is evil: why? The answer which theism gives to this problem, which is an answer rather than a solution, is to trust more totally in God, believing that what to men and women may seem utterly wrong, devoid of meaning or purpose, is nevertheless part of God's ineffable will. The failure to understand evil becomes further evidence of God's infinite superiority, and an occasion for recognizing that any attempt to comprehend God's ways would be folly. One person recalled her own share of suffering:

> My husband was killed in the war and after that I felt that as obviously God did not care why should I? Then after the war I married again – and was happy – then my baby son died and once again the black despair. I think we all have to go through it in some way or another and I still do not really understand why. Better just to accept it as part of life on trust as one has to accept so much on trust – the belief that although everything in the world looks black God is working his purpose out.(40)

Another letter took a harder look at the unfairness of it all, and concluded, not that it was fair, but simply that God is other:

> The Bible seems to say that God, His purposes, His love and His justice are revealed in history. God does not so appear to me, in the generation that knew about Auschwitz. . . . The psalms as a whole do bring out so terribly often the utter desolation of those who trusted to the covenant. They took it to mean, You play fair by Me and I will play fair by you. They thought God would give them support and prosperity and safety. . . . But history has refuted this. God is other. His purposes are not our purposes and His way is hidden in cloud. (102)

If such a belief is achieved it produces an attitude which is surprised by joy, impressed and filled with wonder by it, while sorrow is accepted with resignation and used to deepen the sense of mystery which surrounds God. The answer to the problem posed by evil is to say that it is beyond the grasp of our finite understanding. This is a theodicy in the strict sense.

The conservatism implicit in theism lies not so much in the acceptance of evil as a mystery as in its tendency not to see it as evil at all, but as good. What is evil, after all? it asks; is it not the name we give to that which causes pain and suffering, for there is no such thing as evil outside the context of our own experience? So-called natural disasters such as earthquakes, floods and volcanoes were not disastrous before the advent of *homo sapiens*, but rather the happy events which made the world assume the shape which we now call beautiful and good. If suffering can be made to serve a useful purpose then the evil in it is exorcized, and it becomes good. This, of course, is the happy, but unsatisfactory, ending to the Book of Job, when he accepts his sufferings as an education in the greatness of God and his own smallness. As a prize for having learned his lesson so well he is given twice as many possessions as he had before, living 'an hundred and forty years', and dying old and full of days. To accept pain as an education is to have solved the problem of evil by transforming evil into a kind of good. A letter recounted the way in which this conclusion was reached by one writer:

> 'Your pain is the breaking of the shell that encloses your understanding. Even as the stone of the fruit must break that its heart may stand in the sun, so must you know pain.'
> (Gibran) My 'pain' was in the form of an automobile accident that almost cost me my life, robbed me of the use of one eye, and did cost my sister's life. I had plenty of time to think and I began to recognize the help and support afforded me by my friends as God working through them, and once that recognition is established it is unending. One sees unrelated pieces of life falling into place and a pattern of continuity taking shape, and I know that all this has become real to me because of this recognition. You may call this rationalization, but to me it is theism. I haven't arrived at what I believe by any sudden enlightenment or experience, but by the use of what God has endowed me with, to think and feel with. (995)

Both conclusions – that evil is simply a mystery, and that in a mysterious way it is a source of strength – are contained in the story of Job, and both fit within what is here called theism. Neither conclusion seeks to evade the fact of evil, but neither will allow it to have the last word, for, either way, it is the profoundest of mysteries.

The further one penetrates into theism as a type of religiousness the more clearly does it emerge as a positive, affirmative attitude to life. Its most characteristic feature is the way in which it appreciates the experience of love and beauty and order, and attributes these to the goodness of God; faced with his magnificence, it sees men and women as tiny and of little account. So when it encounters joy, that is reckoned as evidence of the goodness of God; when it encounters suffering, that is accepted, either as a mystery or as good in mysterious form.

Theism is a comparatively silent kind of religiousness, not given to elaborate accounts of itself, and preferring to sing the praises of God's goodness. It is known well enough in the English cultural tradition because it is embodied in the writings of such poets as Browning and Wordsworth. Like exemplarism, however, it is a popular form of religiousness as well, and if corny phrases like 'a real Christian' betray the influence of exemplarism, others, no less clichés, are sure signs of theism, as when people say that they feel closest to God under the 'blue dome of heaven'. We can turn to Hoggart again, for he describes the vague religious sentiment of the working-class culture as well as the religious articulation of ethics.

> Thus religious – or what are thought to be religious – songs are popular, and a singer will pass from a song about love to a religious song and so to what would be called a 'classical' song, with no sense of incongruity in her or the company; the emotional atmosphere gives an all-embracing unity. We might call this the 'Gracie Fields switch', since Miss Fields is its most notable exponent; she can move successfully from a back-yard comic song to a 'classical' or 'classical religious' song such as: 'The Lost Chord' ('Seated one day at the organ/I was weary and ill-at-ease. . . .'), or 'Bless This House' (which has the Home/God tie – 'Bless this house, O Lord we pray/Make it safe by night and day. . . . Bless the hearth ablazing there/- With smoke ascending like a prayer'); and so to 'The Holy City', or 'Ave Maria', or 'The Lord's Prayer'. In the latter category come also 'Oh, for the Wings of a Dove' (of which a recording made by a boy soprano used to be very popular), 'All Through the Night', 'The Old Rugged Cross', and the hymn which more than any other belongs to the working-class, 'Abide with Me': it is sung at football matches and other large public occasions, and many a working-class mother asks only for that at her funeral. My mother did so, and my grandmother some years later; for both of them it had an enormous weight of suggestion, of God as Father, of Heaven as Home, and of the long day of work which had been their lives, drawing to a close.[4]

Hoggart's last sentence points clearly to the character of natural religion with its sense of a larger plan based on a normal lifetime's experience. This too is religion.

When theists come face to face with what is ugly, their response is one whose resonances are all with the Old Testament, rather than the New. Running the full gamut of the emotions which a child knows with its father, one accuses God, reviles him, and is angry with him, one pleads and cries to him – but finally one sinks back into trust, and resigns oneself to accepting a will one knows one can neither challenge nor understand.

This gives the clue to theism's characteristic cognitive style. Whereas exemplarism hopes and conversionism is assured, theism trusts. It is no accident that this comes so close to the ordinary meaning[5] of the verb 'to believe', which has little or nothing to do with assertions that something is so, but expresses a relationship of trust and confidence in another (or the Other), for if there is a type of religiousness which is 'natural' to western culture, and to English culture in particular, it is theism. I do not for a moment claim that it is the commonest religious attitude, for others have certainly occurred with greater frequency, but I would argue that a world-affirming monotheism, in which natural religion outweighs revealed religion in importance, is the norm for the West. The belief of theism is not a 'belief that': it is 'belief in'.

Finally, the inexplicitness of theism is most apparent when it comes to consider what happens after death. It does not know, but it is not anxious, for it trusts that whatever is to be will be good. With J.M. Barrie, it can say cheerfully that to die will be the greatest adventure of all. It is a perfectly coherent type of religiousness, but it displays a marked reluctance to speak its name or to disclose its character. It avoids dogma, and it distrusts any attempt to try to pin it down. It was described eloquently by Hubert Foss, who believed something like it to have been the inspiration of Vaughan Williams's Fantasia on a theme of Thomas Tallis, when he wrote of that piece of music that it held,

the faith of England, in its soil and its traditions, firmly believed yet expressed in no articled details. There is quiet ecstasy and then alongside of it comes a kind of blind persistence, a faithful pilgrimage towards the unseen light.

How would the pure theist, if such a person existed, fare when confronted with the check-list of items on the sociological questionnaire? I think we can assume that there would be a lot of tepid answers and several 'don't knows'. Questions about the virgin birth and the Bodily resurrection of Jesus would barely connect with the respondent's experience. We have touched on public worship in discussing theism's attitudes to the Church and church-going, but private prayer, which would appear as another item on the questionnaire, has not been mentioned. A problem would arise again here: 'Do you pray?' The question is impossibly difficult for the theist to answer, for 'prayer' is a rather churchy word for a conscious sense of wonder.

But theism can be identified. Its general characteristics are an affirmation of the vague and general principles – God, life after death, a meaning to life, a sense of mystery – and an unwillingness to affirm dogmatic articles of faith – Jesus, sin, the Church, salvation. Its particular characteristic is its combination of attitudes to God and to evil and to suffering, for no other type of religiousness will believe implicity in God, and at the same time be disturbed by the problem of evil.

In theism we have a religious style which can be at once passionate and well-nigh invisible, and therefore it is easy to ignore as no more than residual sentiments. Such an analysis would be in error, I think, and its existence merits serious attention.

5   Gnosticism

The fourth type of religiousness we shall examine, which I shall call *gnosticism*,[1] is marked by an overriding concern with 'spiritual' matters, the 'spiritual world'.

Every religion and every type of religiousness has a conception of some order of reality which transcends the material world of tables and chairs. Even exemplarism, which eschews metaphysics, hopes for a future which will radically transcend the present. The transcendent order of reality assumes as many forms as there are types of religion, but although they defy systematic classification, certain broad groups occur, and gnosticism belongs to one such group.

Gnosticism has two main ways in which it is interested in the spiritual world. Firstly, it is greatly concerned with the life after death, and secondly, it believes that we have access to the powers of the spiritual world, which it is anxious to explore and understand. We shall see some of the implications of these two focuses of interest in the course of examining gnosticism, but it is important to grasp from the outset that it is not only the attention paid to the spiritual world which characterizes this type of religiousness, but the degree of attention paid to it. Gnosticism is so exercised by the spiritual world, and so aware of its reality, that the ordinary world known to the five senses is unreal by comparision. 'This creation, or life in matter – the carnal mind – is a mesmeric dream from which we all need to be awakened and over which we have been given domination.' (485) The religion of gnostics gives them the power to discern the true reality. The language which is used can vary, but it always conveys the idea that the unseen reality is readily perceptible to those who have the right knowledge, and that there is nothing spooky about it. It is supernatural, but it is readily accessible. When it is understood aright it is recognized as entirely natural, and supernatural only in the sense of existing on a higher, or at least a different, plane. Different people give the knowledge itself different names, and one letter calls it 'mysticism', and says that it

> should not be confused with pseudo-mysticism, i.e. astrology, witchcraft, numerology and other eccentric cults. The essence of mysticism and the occult is really quite simple. It just means . . . a partial lifting of the veil which divides us from the unseen. Unfortunately this has become overlaid during the course of centuries by a welter of fantasy, exaggeration, mystery-mongering, false doctrine, superstition and mythology – as happens in all religions. (1678)

The note of impatience is characteristic of gnosticism. It sees the existence of a spiritual world as so obvious that it simply cannot understand how people can be blind enough or stupid enough not to acknowledge it. It is impatient, too, with those who obscure the spiritual world with 'superstition and mythology'.

The emphasis on spiritual matters implies, as we have already seen, dismissing the ordinary world. It is a 'mesmeric dream'. Impatient to see beyond the mere surface reality of everyday experience, the gnostic wants to be in touch with the reality beyond. So nature holds no charms for gnostics. On the contrary, nature, the material world, and human nature all have a negative connotation, for they constitute a barrier to the spiritual world. What we should strive for, according to the gnostics, is an understanding of the world along these lines. Modern science can help us to achieve this insight according to some, and one writer cites a specific scientific report:

> I would like to quote here a final paragraph that appeared in, I think, *The Detroit News*. The editorial discusses the latest discoveries into the atom and its constituent parts, saying that with every discovery it is found that the atom is made up of more and more nothingness! 'till matter, so hard to the touch, so cruel to the unwary, is slowly proving to be a transient shadow of ignorance, perhaps'. . . . if God is All in All, then there can be nothing which is material! (1214)

If this is true, then not only are the apparently good and beautiful things no more than a mirage, but so too are the bad and the ugly things in life. And this is the point. The letter just quoted goes on at once to say: 'Sin, sickness, fear and death must be "transient shadows of ignorance" or an illusion!' (1214) This view of the material world proves to be a way of coming to terms with the problem of evil.

The theodicy found in gnosticism approximates to one of the three which, alone, Weber recognized to be consistent, namely dualism.[2] As a religious doctrine, dualism refers to the idea that equal forces of good and evil, light and darkness, etc., are at work in the universe. The way to salvation, within a dualistic view, is to flee from the power of darkness and gain access to the power of light, and this does approximately characterize the attitude of what I am describing here as gnosticism. It deviates from pure dualism in identifying, rather simply, all that is temporal and material with the power of darkness, but this is the deviation which has been common in Christianity from its earliest years through the influence of 'Gnosticism'.[3]

Gnosticism as we find it today is clearly dualistic in its view of the universe as divided into the material or carnal world, and the spiritual world. It is dualistic in its understanding of human nature also, so that someone could write:

> We are made 'in the image and likeness of God', but men
> everywhere try to drag God down to their own littleness. . . .
> In the divine soul of every human being there is perfect peace
> and unalterable goodness, even when in the person there is a
> diseased body and a wicked mind. So we are not really the
> body and nothing more – we are potentially divine. . . . We
> have become so deeply sunk into our bodies and intellects that
> we have lost the habit of remembering what we are and where
> we belong. (1295)

The strict distinction between the divine soul within each one of us, and the 'person' or body which clothes it, provides the gnostic with a way of understanding evil and suffering. These are things which cannot touch our innermost, most essential being. What is wrong is that we fail to 'remember' our true nature. An alternative way of expressing the same idea is to speak in terms not of 'remembering' but of 'higher understanding', as in the following letter:

> As man reaches higher in the understanding of God, and of
> 'the ultimate truth', so the power generally given to sin,
> alcohol, drugs, hypnotism, fear, and all other 'evils' of this
> earth disappear into nothingness. . . . If men can come to a
> full understanding of God, then there can be no evil, disease
> or 'lack of harmony'. (1214)

We shall return to the dualism of gnostics. The point here is that the evil is interpreted as fundamentally unreal by gnosticism. It belongs to the surface of things, and the human task is to penetrate the surface and arrive at the point from which suffering will appear as the sham it really is.

God has already been mentioned in more than one letter which has been quoted. Theism, we saw, is deeply puzzled by how God can allow evil. What is the nature of God for gnostics if their attitude to evil is as has been described? The answer is that, just as our innermost selves are, or should be, above evil, belonging to a spiritual world where evil is unknown, so too is God. Gnosticism, in the words of one letter, has 'a God who is Love and of purer eyes than to *behold* evil. A God who is infinite spirit, intelligence, truth.' (485) The image of God reinforces the gnostic's view that one should not deign to take evil seriously. God does not. Indeed the word 'God' does not refer to anything which could possibly have an attitude towards evil as far as gnostics are concerned. It refers to a principle rather than to a person or a being. 'God' is the name we give to the principle underlying the universe when we understand its true nature. Another letter said 'I would just like to add that now I have found great benefit from thinking of God as omnipresent Love, Mind and Principle and that what passes for evil is counterfeit.' (2445) The consistency of gnosticism is evident. The understanding of human nature, of Creation, of God, all tie in together, and they are all informed by the gnostic's interpretation of evil as belonging to an inferior level of existence. When gnostics talk of our 'carnal bodies' they are not thinking of gluttony and lust as carnal appetites which are 'wrong', but of all which obscures our perception of the spiritual world in which such things simply do not figure. Such notions as 'sin', therefore, need to be abandoned. When we understand life spiritually we realize that there are no such things as 'wrong' or 'evil' or 'pain', or at least nothing positive to be corrected. We should see such things as impediments to a true understanding and as phenomena which must be seen through, as one 'sees through' a person who is pretending to be something he or she is not. A further letter spells this out a little:

> We are all aware of what we call the spirit in man which makes him love the good and the beautiful and there could not be this spirit in man if it were not for the fact that Spirit *is*, and man in his higher nature reflects it and is like it. . . .
> Humanity's approximation to this Principle of Love is found in compassion, in forgiveness, in generosity, patience, unselfishness, sympathetic understanding and so on, but the Principle itself has nothing to forgive, for it always beholds the loveliness of its object, and does not identify it with unloveliness of any kind. I believe, and to some extent have

proved that as this idea of Love is better understood, it knocks
the bottom out of sin and dissolves it. The old idea of a
personal God looking down on the man whom 'He' has
created capable of sinning, and forgiving the sinner but leaving
him free to sin again does not come into the picture. (616)

So the idea of 'sin' disappears. And with it goes any notion of
prayer. One cannot pray unless there is someone or something to
whom a prayer is addressed. Just as sin is reinterpreted as
disharmony with the spiritual world, therefore, prayer is
reinterpreted as the process whereby one purifies one's understanding, lifting one's consciousness above material things to the
spiritual world.

Gnostics have a favourite image for expressing the discon-
tinuity between the material world and the spiritual world. It is
an image drawn from St Paul's second letter to the Church at
Corinth, which expresses the dualism of gnostics very explicitly,
and it is invoked in the following passage from a letter:

St Paul says somewhere that we have a natural body and a
spiritual body. It seems to me that there is a natural universe
obeying physical laws and beloved of astronomers, physicists,
spacemen and the like, and there is a spiritual universe
beloved of poets, mystics, saints and so on. . . . Ordinary man
is so much more than an animal walking about on two legs.
(872)

That passage raises other issues which we must consider, but the
idea of our 'two bodies' which it introduces is of very special
importance. Its significance as an image which expresses a
dualistic view of reality is twofold. In the first place it is popular.
Gnosticism as a type of religiousness was not over-represented in
the letters to Dr Robinson, and indeed its existence was far from
being immediately obvious,[4] but this biblical quotation was
probably invoked more often than any other single quotation.[5]
Since the notion bears no special relevance to what Dr Robinson
had written, its frequent occurrence must be taken to be
significant, not least because it has no great currency in ordinary
conversation as far as I am aware. And in the second place it is
biblical. Most of this style of religiousness involves a radical
reinterpretation of what passes for conventional Christianity, and
therefore its articulation through the use of a biblical phrase calls
for comment. We shall consider the attitude of the gnostic to the
Church presently, but at this point it should be noted that using a
biblical expression, and doing so self-consciously, strongly
suggests that gnosticism thinks of itself quite unambiguously as

religious in the Christian tradition. As we shall see, some gnostics come close to despairing of the Church, but the constant use of what is taken to be a biblical concept makes it plain that gnosticism considers itself an interpretation of Christianity – and the correct interpretation, needless to say – rather than as any kind of alternative.

A passage from one further letter emphasizes the idea of 'two bodies' even more strongly:

> For what it is worth I do not think that the point is pressed home to all, and particularly children, that man has two bodies. One mortal and one spiritual. So it does not matter what happens, in the scheme of things to our Earthly body, for it is the Spiritual body that is seeking shall we say perfection. . . . I think the mass of men and women want a simple answer and simple books to read, particularly about our two Bodies, which point I feel *must* be pressed home. (2046)

The dualistic character of gnosticism is clearly apparent in this distinction not only between the material world and the spiritual world, but in the conception of human nature as being characterized by two distinct bodies.

The last letter but one which was quoted spoke of the 'spiritual universe' as 'beloved' of mystics, among others. This must lead us to ask whether gnosticism, as it is described here, is the type of religiousness embraced by persons in the Christian mystical tradition. At first sight it seems reasonable to suppose this to be the case. The mystic is embarked upon a spiritual quest, and, fleeing the world, seeks to live in the spiritual world of the presence of God. The *via negativa* in Christianity may not regard the world as unreal, but it certainly sees the mystical experience as realizable through the rejection of worldly and carnal things. Furthermore mystics have been thought to have access to supernatural powers and to be capable of levitation and such like activities. Compared with what has been seen of gnosticism so far, the religion of mystics is different, however, in three crucial respects. Firstly, it conceives of God in personal, not abstract, terms, seeing the mystical experience as a personal relationship. Secondly, it regards the 'spiritual life' as the special calling of a few, not the norm, and a special calling, moreover, which is different but not intrinsically superior to others. And thirdly, mystics aim to be unconcerned with mystical experiences as such. Whereas gnostics are wholly preoccupied with the spiritual world, mystics are too absorbed with God, as the goal of their spiritual journey, to be detained by features of the spiritual world through which they pass.[6] It would seem, therefore, that although there are similarities between gnosticism and mysticism, mysticism is so disciplined and refined a form of gnosticism as to be transformed into a distinctly different type of religiousness. If nothing more is said about mysticism here it is because there were no letters from mystics among the letters to Dr Robinson, or at least none about mysticism.

We have seen that the idea of God represents a principle rather than a being or a person for gnostics. We must now examine who and what Jesus is reckoned to be. Relating Jesus to God, one letter put it thus:

> I have always believed that God is a spirit, the spirit of love and goodness, and that Christ was so endued with that spirit, He was the essence of God – the *real* man is not the outward form, but the inner spirit. (1195)

We must note that in defining the nature of Jesus, human nature has to be mentioned again. On this account, Jesus represents a supreme example, and since all human beings are 'really' spirit rather than body, Jesus was all spirit. The dualism of body and spirit runs right through gnosticism: we ordinary human beings are spirit clothed with flesh; God is pure spirit; Jesus, as a human being, was so lightly clothed with flesh that the spirit was plainly visible. The terminology people use to express this basic dualism varies. Another letter positively denies the idea of spirit, sensing that it smacks too much of concepts such as individual, person, and being, and thus tends to obscure the fact that God is pure principle:

> No spirit, God is individualised in every one of us, the potential Christ, for the Christ is no man but the divine principle or Light in every human being, and Jesus was manifesting an individuality of this divine principle to a superlative degree. (617)

This is another way of saying that Jesus was an example of what human nature can be at its highest, but without imputing a purpose to God there is a strong suggestion that Jesus was in some sense 'sent' to show others the way. Another letter elaborates the idea that we are all Christs, and that Jesus was *the* Christ in that he represented the summit of humanity:

> All men are incarnate 'Sons of God'. Every birth is an incarnation, every life a spiritual crucifixion, every death a spiritual ascension. What is wrong, it seems to me, is that we try to set up Christ as a creature from some other supernatural

'plane' completely divorced from our own experience of natural life. As Christ is, *so are we all*. We are all spiritual beings incarnate in a natural world. (872)

Were it not for the last sentence in that quotation it might have been taken as an illustration of exemplarism. Both types of religiousness do indeed see Jesus as having been the same kind of creature as ourselves, but the different doctrines of human nature which characterize exemplarism and gnosticism ensure that the doctrines of Christ, too, are radically different. Here Jesus is more than an example, however, for his life appears almost as the type of all human life. The mention of death, which is interpreted as 'ascension', anticipates our examination of gnosticism's views on the life after death, but we have here another expression of the basic gnostic position with its characteristic dualism.

It will be apparent that there is a certain affinity between this type of religiousness and ideas expounded by Spiritualism,[7] and we shall consider those connections shortly. A letter from someone influenced by Spiritualism sheds some further light on how gnosticism regards Jesus, however, and also anticipates our discussion of the nature of belief as it is known to gnostics:

Jesus was a son of God like we are sons and daughters of God. We have been told he was a voluntary incarnation into this world. He came to teach us how to live and heal. Greater things will ye do than this He said. (519)

That quotation contains a suggestion of Christian Science, too, which is another movement which contains a preponderant element of what I am calling gnosticism.

Despite its stress on the spirit which is so much more than the body, gnosticism includes a belief in personal survival after death. I say 'despite', because it might seem more consistent for gnostics to believe that after death they will be re-absorbed into the one Spirit. The reason this is not so is that the gnostic belief in the unreality of the body and the natural world is rooted in the problem of evil. The concept of salvation as a release from existence, or at least from individual existence, which is common in the religions of the East, implies a belief in the worthlessness of material and temporal existence. While there are superficial similarities between this view and the view of gnosticism they are in fact very different. Gnosticism does not reject 'existence'. Instead it cuts 'existence' clearly into two, and denigrates one half in order that it may experience the other. Religious traditions of the East are convinced of the futility of existence, *per se*; gnosticism is revolted by our present existence. The repeated references to sin, pain, disease, wickedness, and so on make it clear that gnosticism rejects the carnal body and the material world because they are the arena of evil. It seeks the spiritual body and the spiritual world because they transcend evil, but so far from amounting to non-existence they 'are' much more, and are more immediately real to the gnostic. The survival of the spirit within each human being is therefore a natural part of gnosticism. Expressed in very simple terms, the following letter, which is quoted in its entirety, states clearly the gnostic belief in a spiritual life which awaits us.

> I can tell you that there is another, and better, world for us when God calls us from this world. It's only our bodies that die, not our souls, which I can prove. My daughter, aged 19, passed away from this earth 20 years ago, 1944, but I have seen her, in spirit, since, and she looks very well and happy. I have also seen other members of my family too and they are all well and happy and they all look happy and younger, and are dressed, just like we are, in ordinary clothes. I could tell you a lot, only it would take so much time. I am not a spiritualist or a Catholic, but I just know that when we leave this earth we continue our lives in the next, but we leave all our aches and pains like I've got and worries here. I can prove what I say. I can't understand how any real Christian could doubt it after the Resurrection of Christ. I don't pretend to be a very good Christian, I don't go to Church or read the bible now but I do believe in God and He has been with me all through my life. I am 62 now, and a widow, without God's help I would not be as well as I am (could be a lot better) but I'm putting my trust in God and when he decides to call me I'll be glad to go as I know I'll be free from pain and worries and will see all my friends and relations again. I'm looking forward to it. (2839)

This touchingly simple account of a belief held with utter conviction contains few of the speculations or ideas which are characteristic of gnosticism. It serves to illustrate the gnostic view because it contains the clear idea of the soul or spirit being detachable from an inferior body, because the idea is firmly grounded in the experience of evil, and because the idea is based on knowledge rather than belief.[8]

The writer of the last letter quoted said that she was 'not a spiritualist or a Catholic'. The linking of the two suggests that the woman thought of herself as ordinary and unexceptional, and as not belonging to any group with 'funny' beliefs. As a disclaimer, it is of considerable interest to the sociologist of religion, but while that particular correspondent was not a Spiritualist, a few others were, and a number expressed sympathy or support for the ideas of Spiritualism. Thus one person said:

> Spiritualism is the discovery of natural laws, nothing mysterious about it. . . . When we pass out of our natural body we only change our state, we live in a different vibration (much quicker). We have been told by highly evolved spirits. (519)

We shall return to 'vibrations' and the like, but the point to note about the influence of Spiritualism is that it is seen as contributing factual knowledge to our religious understanding: 'nothing mysterious about it'. The issue which is immediately raised is the attitude of gnostics to the Church, for it is particularly clear in the relationship between Spiritualism and the Church.

Gnostics themselves see nothing in their beliefs which is contrary to the Church's teaching. They know that their particular interpretation of the Christian religion is unusual, but any disapproval seems to them unreasonable. One person expressed simple puzzlement: 'The Church has always eschewed such speculations and looked upon them almost as wrong. Why I don't know.' (3203) The characteristic attitude of gnosticism, however, is more impatient than that. Gnostics typically see an urgent need for the Church to learn what it can about spiritual matters, and they regard their own insights as of special value. So another person wrote:

> Do you not think that if only the Church was in real communion with the Unseen World . . . a real understanding of how those who have died live in this next phase of life would enable it to combat the great materialism of this age. (1204)

In fact the Churches have come to take quite an active interest in the things which concern gnostics. There are people and groups with ecclesiastical approval who concern themselves with spiritual healing, spiritualism and psychical research in general, and so on. So it was possible for a clergyman to write:

> It seems to me that Spiritualism (at its best) gives a coherent, exciting and rationally attractive picture of life after death – a picture which centres round the opportunity for further development. They also describe the survival of a spiritual, or psychic, body which preserves the personality in recognizable form. (2755)

What is significant is that the 'knowledge' of gnosticism is purely factual and therefore in no way at variance with religion. E.M. Forster portrayed the gnostic attitude in a character in his novel, *Maurice*.

> The old gentleman employed his leisure in evolving a new religion – or rather a new cosmogony, for it did not contradict chapel. The chief point was that God lives within the sun, whose bright envelope consists of the spirits of the blessed. Sunspots revealed God to man, so that when they occurred Mr Grace spent hours at his telescope noting the interior darkness. The incarnation was a sort of sunspot. . . . [The opinions] were those of the practical man who tries to think spiritually – absurd and materialistic, but first hand.

Gnosticism's attitude to the Church is marked by impatience, but it is not negative. Almost everything in the Christian religion requires some adjustment or reinterpretation, but scripture contains ample material to assist the gnostic. Any incipient hostility is avoided because gnosticism is concerned with studying straightforwardly factual matters which do not contradict the Church, but supplement its teaching, providing it with a more satisfactory gloss and generally bringing it up to date.

This brings us to gnosticism's understanding of 'belief'. Someone wrote: 'In the long run I don't really believe in anything myself – except God – and hard facts.' (1678) The characteristic cognitive style of this type of religiousness, as will already have become apparent, is 'knowledge'. The gnostic is not content to believe, but wants to know. One person recounted the experience of coming to realize the need for knowledge rather than belief.

> Before the last war *I believed* in God. This was due, of course, to something like twenty years attendance at a Congregational Church . . . but! On leaving the Army I found I had believed because it was 'the thing to do', but my belief had no substance. If I pricked it I found that I had *no faith*, that it would burst in my face. So I realised that belief and faith had to go a step further – for me at any rate. I had to know, *to understand*, to prove, and that I think is most urgently needed today. (2445)

One striking corollary to the 'scientific' cognitive style of gnosticism is that beliefs tend to be expressed in the terms of science, after the fashion of Forster's Mr Grace. Because there is 'nothing mysterious' about the religious knowledge of gnosticism it seeks to express itself in the language of physical science. Someone writing about our destiny in the spiritual world, therefore, could express it in quasi-evolutionary terms: 'the material of our fleshly robes was once mineral, later plant and animal, and is now human, later divine'. (1295) Just as popular as the language of evolution to express the relationship between the material and the spiritual, and more striking because of its overtly scientific character, is the idea that matter vibrates at different rates, as we have seen already. Thus another correspondent could write:

> Science has proved that all matter vibrates and the vibrations cover a certain scale. . . . Obviously if we pursue this scientific fact it becomes reasonably easy to realise that it is more or less obvious that in higher (or lower) vibrations life can and does exist – that all around us the higher vibration of spirit is present though neither heard nor seen without special gifts or abilities, i.e. psychic gifts. (117)

The language reinforces the factual character of the religious knowledge of gnosticism. Whether based on first-hand experience or on knowledge received from others, this type of religiousness has knowledge, rather than belief.

We have seen in gnosticism a further way of being religious which is not accurately assessed except in its own terms. The traditional criteria of religiousness in the Christian tradition will evoke comparatively weak responses from the gnostic, but expressed in slightly different terms they may expose religious views which are indeed deeply held.

6 Traditionalism

Are we to understand that Christianity is no more than a moral code based on total love, preached by a Christ who was no more than the selfless, brilliant, illegitimate son of a poor carpenter? Is only the Crucifixion an historical truth? Are the Resurrection, the Ascension, the Holy Ghost no more than myths? If so, what truths are they supposed to reveal? In a world of shifting values and total insecurity, is there no divine power on whom we can call to give us the strength and courage to meet its menace? Is there no Christ of Atonement to conquer for us the sin we cannot conquer unaided, no after-life where we will be joined with those we love? . . . We feel miserable and abandoned and more than anything in the world yearn for the God who, it seems, was too good to be true.

Having outgrown the God of our childhood, where do we look for the God on whom we lean in our adult years? What truths can we convey with complete conviction to our children on the threshold of their lives? They are looking to us for assurances we find we can no longer give with confidence. (6)

I'm sick of the voice of the Church which gives men and women the right to think and live as they please – surely this is the reason the world is in the mess it's in. (701)

So far we have seen four contrasting ways of being religious. They are so different from each other that they look almost like four religions, although we must remember that they might not look so distinctively different to someone from a non-Christian culture. Each type of religiousness has been presented as having its own mode of belief, or cognitive style. A distinct focus of concern has been identified for each: Jesus, the experience of having been saved, God, and the spiritual world. The final type of religiousness which I shall examine, and which I call *traditionalism*, has no characteristic object of belief or experience. Its lack of any single, defining focus makes it appear at first to be unlike the previous four types, but in fact this lack is its own distinguishing feature. It is not a lack at all, but a positive characteristic.

I shall use very few extracts from the letters to illustrate traditionalism and therefore two quotations stand at the head of the chapter. They should help to introduce this type of religiousness. It would not have been difficult to find illustrative quotations, but their inclusion would have helped the discussion little since the sentiments would have been too familiar. Traditionalism believes in everything conventionally included in the Christian religion, and since the substance of its beliefs is so well-known I shall not rehearse it, but concentrate on the style of believing which, while it is not unknown, is less well appreciated.

Durkheim defined religion as a system of beliefs and practices which unite believers into a community.[1] That is to say, he disregarded the question of what beliefs and practices may properly be called religious, and shifted attention to the question of the function performed by those beliefs and practices which we describe as religious. Religious beliefs, for him, were defined not by what they are, but by what they do. Recognizing the variety of objects regarded as sacred by different peoples, and the range of religious attitudes, he proposed as the lowest common denominator of all religions the power of beliefs and practices to bind together all those who share them. What struck him most forcibly about religion was its obligatory character. Writing about the France of his own day, in the midst of the Dreyfus Affair, when the authority of Catholicism was much weakened and yet when certain ideas and institutions could still command universal respect among Frenchmen, he said:

> We know today that a religion does not necessarily imply
> symbols and rites in the full sense, or temples and priests. All
> this external apparatus is merely its superficial aspect.
> Essentially, it is nothing other than a system of collective
> beliefs and practices that have a special authority.[2]

Now this may or may not be an accurate account of what is 'truly' religious, but it should be immediately apparent that most of what passes for religion in our own day has exactly the opposite quality. Each of the four types of religious attitude described so far is voluntary, not compulsory, and so on Durkheim's view none is properly regarded as religious. He himself suggested that the religion which had emerged at the end of the nineteenth century centred on the sanctity and inviolability of the individual, whose rights and whose dignity were alone regarded as above discussion.[3] Thomas Luckmann, one of the few social scientists to have restated Durkheim's position, argues that the religion of the Churches is effectively dead, and, in a more pessimistic mood than Durkheim ever adopted, he suggests that the notions which in our culture are sufficiently obligatory to merit being called 'religious' are such things as individual autonomy, self-expression, self-realization, the mobility ethos, sexuality, and family centredness.[4] I mention the Durkheimian perspective because this fifth type of religiousness, unlike the previous four, is experienced as having precisely this quality of obligatoriness. In examining it in some detail what will be striking, I think, will be the necessity of believing, rather than what is believed. A similar quality was remarked upon in the discussion of conversionism. I suggested that the insistence with which conversionists will affirm the truth of a range of beliefs should be interpreted as a series of re-affirmations of the central experience of having been saved. In the case of traditionalism there is no focal point, but the general tenor of affirmation is as striking as with conversionism. Its significance will become clear in the course of the discussion.

The essence of traditionalism as a style of religion is that it cherishes the tradition which it has received. It may be simply appreciative, wishing to affirm all it has known as good, or it may be aggressive, defending belligerently its security. Although superficially different, these are no more than moods evoked by different external circumstances. They are the responses made by one type of religiousness to a variety of situations, ranging from defensive postures, through relaxed moods, to postures of attack.

Conservation is an idea which is in vogue at the present time, but what it stands for is far from new. Long before anyone talked of conservation the farmer, for example, was a conservationist. Good farmers know every inch of their land: they appreciate its needs and its potential, they care for it, and they are concerned that when they hand on their farms they should be as good as when they received them, and if possible better. Keeping a farm in good order is an end in itself, worth doing for its own sake, and although the value of a property may be increased or its profitability rise, such things were incidental to the best traditional farmer, whose main concern was conservation. The craftsman, too, is a conservationist when he receives, guards, and passes on a skill, for craftsmanship demands patient respect for traditional wisdom and skills. This spirit of conservation finds ready expression in religion, for religious tradition accords well with the pattern of receiving, cherishing, and handing on. Just as it takes a lifetime for the farmer to know his land and how to care for it, or the joiner to become a skilled craftsman, so a lifetime may be spent learning for oneself the wisdom accumulated over countless generations and enshrined in a religious tradition. In a traditional culture, religion is the quintessence of the stable and secure pattern of receiving, preserving, and handing on, and, furthermore, it constitutes a framework within which the pattern is accepted as universal and God-given. In more tangible ways, too, religion stands as the epitome of the established order of life. Church buildings have traditionally been intended to last for ever, or at any rate for many centuries, and the rite with which both buildings and their contents are consecrated sets them apart and hallows them for ever. Even the organizational officers of a Church, the bishops or ministers, are ordained or consecrated for life. A secure and unchanging pattern of life, then, is the very essence of religion. The absolute character of religious truths and the changeless quality of religious buildings, the religious organization, religious music and forms of religious worship, all epitomize tradition and guarantee it.

Traditionalism is a style of religiousness which holds to the old ways. What has been described as the essence of religion in the preceding paragraph may seem quaint and out of date, but for the traditionalist it remains the norm.

One can see readily enough that for this type of religious attitude every single element in its tradition is important. Each detail has a unique and familiar place in the pattern as a whole, and so if any particular is threatened or called into question it is the pattern itself which is put at risk, for it is the stability of the whole pattern which is sacred; herein lies the peculiarity and the distinctiveness of traditionalism as a type of religiousness. And a distinctive cognitive style goes with traditionalism. The attitude is one of unquestioning acceptance, of taking for granted, and yet of sincerely appreciating the religious traditions. We understand what traditionalists mean when they say, 'I believe', if we take them to be saying 'I cherish and hold dear'.[5] The cognitive style involves no assertion of truth, and implies no doubt. Thus the way in which traditionalists believe is distinctively different from the ways in which the previous four styles of religiousness believe.

As we normally encounter it, traditionalism expresses itself with a self-assurance which is unable to conceive of doubt or of contradiction. When traditionalists encounter unbelief they regard it as sad, or bad, or mad, but they do not take it seriously. You cannot ask traditionalists, therefore, to explain what they believe, or why they believe it. They find that they simply cannot tell you what they believe and the best they can do is to recite the creed, or to quote a verse from the Bible, or to mention some lines from a favourite hymn. The problem of why they believe is more difficult still. They tend to treat the very question with incredulity, and say, 'The same yesterday, today, and for ever', or invoke some other such saying to express the conviction that things just are so, and could not conceivably be otherwise.

When in England a bishop of the Established Church says that he thinks it unlikely that Jesus physically ascended into the sky and may not physically have risen from the grave, that a meal shared with friends may be as holy as Holy Communion and that fornication need not invariably be wrong, then even self-assured traditionalists feel compelled to take seriously the implicit questions, What do you believe? and, Why do you believe it? When forced to express itself, traditionalism can be articulated in more moods than one, as I have suggested. When one is personally threatened there is not a straight choice as to whether one will either capitulate or fight: some will sadly resign themselves to injury, some will attack their assailant vigorously, some will attempt forcibly to restrain the person who attacks them as someone who must be deranged. Similarly traditionalism responds in a variety of ways, and the traditionalism which is represented in the letters addressed to Dr Robinson is expressed, as one would expect, in tones of distress, disgust, and dismay. If religion is seen as a symbol of changelessness and security then any threat to religion will be regarded as an outrage which threatens to undermine that security, and it will seem all the more outrageous if the threat comes from a bishop – from one who has been appointed to be a custodian of the religious tradition. The first of the two quotations at the beginning of this chapter expresses the sad distress experienced by some people when doubts arise. What is striking about traditionalism, and what is illustrated by that quotation, is that religion is a matter of all or nothing. Life is at risk of falling apart altogether unless the whole tradition is true.

While a religion is a total way of life rather than a set of ideas, every religion does also contain a set of answers to certain recurring questions. If religions differ from one another that is because, amongst other things, some particular question may be of predominant importance, and an answer to it may colour the whole religious attitude. We saw, for example, that the limits imposed by death, disease and human perception may force the question of what lies beyond those limits, and that gnosticism answers the question by affirming a spiritual reality which is opposed to material reality. Each type of religious attitude which has been described has its own particular central question, and an appropriately elaborated answer. In the last chapter I suggested that gnosticism deals with the problem of evil by treating it as part of a world which is sub-natural in comparison with the world of the spirit. Its theodicy is based on a dualistic view of the universe so that God cannot be accused of allowing evil to affect us. 'Why should this happen?' is not a question which gnostics address to God. Gnosticism prevents the question from being a problem by making sure that it is never asked, and thus, in a sense, it is an efficient form of religiousness. Given the right social conditions, traditionalism is more efficient still, and is much the most efficient type of religiousness of the five described here, if we use 'efficient' in the same sense. It has an answer to no question in particular, but in its own special way it is able to prevent any troubling question from being asked at all. Traditionalism consists of a series of beliefs and practices which shield the believer from ever being troubled by questions by defining the whole of experience as unproblematical.

There is a traditional way of doing anything one cares to think of. In every stable culture there is a recipe for every situation and a prescribed solution to every problem, be it great or small, and in large part it is the ready acceptance of these recipes and solutions which renders such societies stable. When a problem leads unavoidably to the need to decide between two incompatible courses of action (shall we wage war, or not?) there is a prescribed way in which to decide, such as divination or the drawing of lots, and there are no problems which do not have their own traditional solutions. In a similar way there are no questions which do not have their own traditional answers, and in traditional, stable cultures it is difficult to draw a line between the religious and the secular: all is a matter of tradition, and tradition is all. Traditionalism, either secular or religious, makes life easy by providing an exhaustive and definitive set of recipes for life, but only – and this defines the 'right conditions' in which traditionalism is so efficient a type of religiousness – in a society which is highly stable.

Although few people in the western world today may be said to live even in pockets of traditional culture, for most of us there are segments of life, at least, in which we are traditional. In theory, a traditional solution or answer is usually available to us, but it is a real option only if it is self-evidently right, for traditional solutions are convincing precisely because no alternative seems credible.[6] The so-called ultimate problems of the meaning of life and death, of good and evil, which conventionally define the area of religious problems, constitute one of those segments of life within whose boundaries traditionalism may reign for some people, and the problems are thereby rendered unproblematical. A whole structure of belief and practice will exist which is a matter of habit and routine. When one of these so-called ultimate problems is encountered it is, as it were, referred to religion, which provides an answer. Because solutions and answers are known to exist, however, the questions do not actually pose problems in any serious sense. Rites of passage provide the clearest examples of this mechanism at work. Some degree of anxiety generally accompanies a person's coming to adulthood and to marriage, the experience of a birth and of a death, and whether the anxiety is resolved in happiness or in grief there is always a tendency to look for an explanation. Religious tradition takes these events and surrounds them with ritual, and by endowing the ritual with supernatural meanings and explanations which locate the experience of the particular event within a larger story, it makes it part of a larger pattern of meaning. By prescribing a marriage ritual, for example, the meaning of the event is prescribed – for the couple, for all those present, and for the couple again through their awareness that those present have expectations which follow from the meaning of the event. The rite provides answers to questions before they have even been asked. It places the unique event in a larger context, thereby assuring the people involved that the questions and anxieties which inevitably accompany a unique event have been faced before, and that it's 'alright'.[7] The strength of traditionalism as a style of religiousness is that it conveys the feeling that all problems do have a solution, and it does this by rehearsing the solutions in solemn fashion as though everyone, for all time, has known them to be true.

What I am calling traditionalism is a true type of religiousness, for although it has no specific content its distinctive feature is its form. In the context of the West, however, and of England in particular, traditionalism has its proper content as well as its universal form. Even within England the content varies since there are Roman Catholic and Methodist traditionalisms as well as the traditionalism which holds dear the orthodox formulations of the Church of England. Church-going is an obligatory practice, though considerable laxity is readily tolerable; the Church as an organization is indispensible and it is represented at a national level by the bishops who sit in the House of Lords and are concerned with matters of state, as their subordinates are at the civic and rural levels. It is of the greatest importance to traditionalism that the Church's presence should be felt and that constant reaffirmations of its role should be made in everyday life, and the clergy are indispensible for this. The clergy are not only the guardians of religion but are themselves religious symbols every bit as palpably as are cathedrals and parish churches. Christian morality also forms an integral part of the pattern, not as a set of abstract principles but as clear and definite rules which are easily grasped, and the traditionalist believes that the law of the land should embody the teachings of the Church. Other parts of the religious institution are similarly regarded as important, though some of them may seem to be trivial in themselves: traditionalism prizes Sunday Schools, and sets great store by the compulsory provision of religious education in state schools; it is even concerned when the BBC proposes to cease broadcasting Choral Evensong on the Home Service at four o'clock on Wednesday afternoons.[8]

The power of traditionalism as a religious attitude lies in its completeness as a pattern of prescribed rules and beliefs. It provides a total context in which decisions and perplexities and pains are given a meaning. You do not have to search out the meaning: your task is to receive and accept it. But the total and all-embracing character of traditionalism is not only its strength, it is its weakness as well, since the questioning of one particular throws the whole thing into doubt. Tradition is the source of certainty, but if the tradition should be wrong in any one particular then the whole structure is shaken and it becomes unreliable in all other particulars.

One letter has been quoted to illustrate the extent of the distress which can be caused when the traditional pattern is shaken. The train of thought runs thus: If Jesus was not God, then how can I bring up my family and how can I live my life? There is a converse train of thought which is no less important, however, for there are some traditionalists who have a skeleton in the cupboard, and if someone breaches the tradition in one particular and then finds, contrary to expectations, that the rest of the pattern remains intact, then that person is left with a guilty secret. It may be that someone has been divorced and remarried, or has secretly rejected the virgin birth of Jesus. The result is a permanent perplexity which asks how it is possible that the pattern of tradition can be breached, and yet that the whole thing has not collapsed. So while many may find their entire world shaken by a bishop who questions the proposition that Jesus ascended bodily into the skies, there are others who, themselves having doubted that very thing all their lives, find their world whole and intact again when, on the authority of a bishop, they learn that there is nothing wrong with having such doubts. Whether the tradition a person cherishes is undermined by some doubt, or restored by that doubt being made legitimate, the implications are the same: the total pattern of beliefs, practices, and moral rules remains intact as a type of religious attitude. Before considering other aspects of traditionalism let us take one last look at the dismay which doubt may cause, expressed in the following letter with a simplicity granted only to the young and the old:

> I am an old person of eighty-six, and my parents brought all the family up to believe in the teaching of Jesus as told in the four gospels. I have not read your book *Honest to God* in fact and could not take it in if I did read it as I could not follow the talk in *Meeting Point* on BBC when you were discussing it. I must belong to that class that Jesus said – except ye become as little children ye cannot enter the Kingdom of Heaven. But I would like to ask you if you would truthfully say yes or no to the following questions? Is it true that God so loved the world that he sent his only beloved son that whosoever believeth in Him should not perish but have everlasting life? And that He said – In my Father's house are many mansions, I go to prepare a place for you? Do you believe that Christ was born of the Virgin Mary? That he died and rose again? and do you believe in the Day of Judgement? A lot of old people are very worried over the controversy on religion, and would like assurance from the heads of the church. (610)

A simple assurance is sought: that God and all that God stands for are the same today as always, and that everything will remain stable and secure.

I have argued that this type of religious attitude is vulnerable to an attack on any aspect of its belief since it is the overall pattern which is important. That proposition needs to be somewhat qualified, however, for there are two points at which traditionalism as a type of Christian religiousness may be especially vulnerable. The first point is belief about Jesus Christ, and the second is the authority of the Bible.

In the first letter to the Church at Corinth St Paul wrote, 'If Christ be not raised, your faith is vain.' Without doubt this belief is important in the Christian religion, but it is of special importance to traditionalism as a type of religious attitude. It was suggested above that traditionalism cannot easily state what it believes or why it believes it. In a wholly traditional culture the reasons for belief in the tradition need never be examined, but they must inevitably be pondered when traditionalism lives alongside scepticism and, as a rule, one point gets singled out as the linchpin of tradition and thereafter it becomes the symbol and final authority for the tradition as a whole. The resurrection of Jesus from the dead has been so treated in Christian traditionalism, and for some believers this historical fact has become the crux of the whole tradition and the proof which is often given as the reason for belief. Now it could be that there are reasons internal to the structure of the Christian religion which make the bodily resurrection decisive for the truth or falsity of Christianity, but, whether this is so or not, it is clear that for some Christians the belief has been accorded its preeminent status for extrinsic reasons. It is clear because those who cite the resurrection as irrefutable evidence clearly are convinced believers anyway, and the evidence is produced for the benefit of others. When confronted with the question, 'Why do you believe?' there are some who, while not wishing to, feel themselves constrained to make some kind of reply, and this assertion of the historicity of the resurreciton has come to be a common defence of traditionalism: it is a flag to wave and a slogan to shout. The reasons why the resurrection should have become so important a belief are not difficult to recognize. The empirical tradition in British culture, and the respect for empirically based ideas which makes the temper of British intellectual tradition so distinctive, predispose the British to appeal to something empirical even when explaining their religious beliefs. The result has been what amounts to an obsession with the idea that Christianity is an 'historical religion', in which the historical fact of the resurrection of Jesus from the dead has been made the key-stone. This belief, then, is especially vulnerable to attack because it has been proclaimed as proof of the truth of Christianity.

The authority of the Bible is the other belief to which traditionalists appeal. 'Because the Bible says so' is a sufficient reason for many people to give when asked to explain a belief or a practice or a moral precept. The way in which this is another symbol and guarantee of the authority of tradition is illustrated by the following passage from a letter:

> I was brought up in the Anglican faith and was a Soloist for over 40 years and in all my years in the service of my great and wonderful creator I have never heard such outright blasphemy coming from the lips of those who should be striving to bolster our faith in the Scriptures, instead of tearing the word of God apart and trying to make us believe it a myth. . . . II Peter

> i.20-21 tells us that all the Scriptures were inspired by God. Jer. x.10 tells us the Lord is the true God. He would not mislead his people by myths. . . . I wonder, does modern science discredit the flood in Noah's day also? Is it any wonder that our young people have gone haywire over the Beatles and people of questionable character such as Christine Keeler etc. Our young people just don't know what to believe in any more (1643)

Biblical fundamentalism is a belief which can appear in many contexts. It is embraced by the kind of religiousness which I have called conversionism, for example, but there it is of subsidiary importance since the grounds for belief are in the experience of conversion. Its paramount significance for traditionalism is symbolic: as with belief in the bodily resurrection of Jesus, the final authority of the Bible is expressive of a whole traditional pattern of which it is a part.

Traditionalism as a type of religious attitude is marked by a certainty which is unquestioning. It is not only certain, it is delighted by its certainty, for the stable and secure order which it knows is something to guard and cherish. It affirms and reinforces the present structure of society, resisting every innovation. It is unconcerned with abstract principles and interested only in applications. Principles are a positive hindrance, indeed, for they exist to justify particular beliefs, practices or precepts, which need no such external authentication, and therefore principles constitute a threat to traditionalism, whose very essence is unquestioning acceptance. The spirit of conservation which characterizes traditionalism is *ipso facto* conservative. Unlike theism, from which social conservatism follows as a consequence, traditionalism actually entails social conservatism, of which it is part and parcel. In so far as traditionalism is prominent as a type of religious attitude in the Churches, religion is a simple expression of conservatism. It is not its spirit, as theism may be argued to be, but its solemn expression. Nor is it simply the mechanism of inertia which checks particular changes, for since the main thrust of traditionalism is to keep a whole religious tradition intact it is necessarily opposed to any change and is always on the alert to press any attempt at innovation back into the established mould.

The ways in which, when it cannot suppress change, traditionalism manages to meet specific changes, disarm them and make allies of them, are many and complex. There are numerous examples of this in religious history and there is no reason to doubt that radical changes in belief, if they were not effectively prevented, would meet the same fate again at the hands of traditionalism. Referring to the way in which radical theology was being received by the traditional religious institutions, Peter Berger wrote in 1967:

> We strongly suspect that this process of neutralization is already taking place as these 'challenging new insights' are integrated in various ecclesiastical programs. In this process there is nothing to prevent the 'death of God' from becoming but another program emphasis, which, if properly administered, need not result in undue disturbances in the ongoing life of the institution.[9]

That process within the religious institution has its equivalent in the religious attitude, for the most striking feature of a certainty which is shaken by one conscientious doubt is the integrity of its total structure. The implicit plea which underlies traditionalism is not for questions to be answered, but for all questioning to be taken away and put under the lock and key of a trustworthy authority.

It is no accident that each of the few letters quoted in this chapter has contained some mention of the confusion and disarray of contemporary society. Traditionalism as a type of religious attitude is intimately connected with a conservative attitude towards social and personal affairs, and here, as in matters of belief, the basis of certainty is found in the willingness to accept tradition, to respect it, and guard it jealously. A letter from a clergyman expressed this point explicitly:

> It seems to me that the worst feature of *Honest to God* and also of your television appearances is the appalling harm they have done to pastoral work in this country and the immensely more difficult burden they have put on parish priests.
>
> From the pastoral point of view *Lady Chatterley's Lover* has done immense harm. You did a great deal in bringing about a sale of $3\frac{1}{2}$ million copies.[10] However you may try to pretend it is a good book, yet the effect on ordinary people has been bad.
>
> Your book *Honest to God* and the newspaper article which gave your interpretation of it have given people the impression that the old ideas of God are only fit for the scrapheap. I am not saying that this was your intention, but what I am saying about the effect is only too true. Indeed I consider you to have done more harm to the pastoral work of the ordinary parish priest than anyone has ever done before. You have given the impression that you despise the ordinary old-fashioned

Christian. To show contempt for the ordinary Christian and
the ordinary parish priest is about the worst thing that a bishop
or parish priest can do.

Worst of all in my opinion was your short appearance in
that BBC Sunday television programme in which you started
off by once more commending *Lady Chatterley's Lover* as
giving the true attitude to sex, then praising Vidler's television
appearance and finally saying how much you enjoyed *That
Was the Week That Was* (where the most sacred beliefs of
Roman Catholics and Jews were held up to ridicule). I saw
Vidler's television performance and it was really nasty. He
said he had no use for parsons and his voice was horribly full
of contempt. He also had no use for ordinary services. For a
priest to have contempt for his fellow-clergy, who have
parishes, is about as low as a priest can descend. . . .

It is not so much what you have written that is bad, but
what appears to me the most horrible and evil attitude of
contempt and superiority to ordinary decent Christians. (1230)

The 'ordinary', of course, is what is traditional; and contempt is
the opposite of the attitude which traditionalism demands.

Concern with morality is of the deepest importance for
traditionalism. The overriding need is for a fixed set of rules, and
their absolute necessity is more vital than anything else. The
point can be made by quoting another letter:

You say that the Church's attitude to homosexuality has
undergone the same transition as that to capital punishment. I
do hope that the government will not catch up with the Church
– if she has altered about homosexuality. Also I do not agree
with the abolition of capital punishment. It would be alright if
the people sentenced were in for life. We had a case here of a
man who murdered a girl about 17. Then he went to a country
town and shot and killed another girl and wounded a school
mistress while they were in the Chapel at prayers. He was let
out of a mental hospital, after the first murder. With regard to
homosexuality it is a perversion. Many small boys have
probably been coerced or even just raped like little girls these
days. After all Sodom was destroyed because of that sin.

I know you keep coming back to Love being stronger than
the law. But what do you mean by love? It seems that your
idea of love is to give people things, regardless of whether it is
right or wrong. Love is caring for people. And divorce is not
caring for your partner. It is a pity the divorced were received
at Buckingham Palace. I feel that so many marriages would
have been saved if it was not so easy to get divorced. Many

children saved endless mental agony. To do that it is sometimes kinder to resist giving in to them.

I know what you are trying to get at. To me your ideas seem so muddled and wooly. I do not *like* capital punishment myself, but if that man had been hanged the school girl would have been alive today. The teacher and the rest of the girls are probably scarred for the rest of their lives in their minds.

I do think that something should be done about the Church of England. The priests are allowed too much latitude. We have men here who preach against the miracles. If you don't believe in miracles you can't be a Christian, I feel, as Christ's birth was a miracle and he said, 'If you can't believe in me believe in my works.'

PS When if ever do you think Fornication is right? Don't you believe that Christ is God? (1669)

While particular offences may cause disgust and horror it is the fear of uncertainty which is most powerfully conveyed in the letter quoted above, and in the second quotation at the beginning of the chapter. What differentiates traditionalism from all other styles of religiousness is the obligatory nature of the prescribed beliefs. Even when appeal is made to the authority of the Bible or to the conclusive proof of the 'empty tomb' it is the same kind of certainty which is thereby established. The whole corpus of beliefs, practices and values have about them the quality of the sacred. There can be no question of degrees of belief in this type of religious attitude: it is all or nothing.

Yet again we have seen a style of religiousness here which deserves to be identified as something distinctive. To describe the traditionalist as being 'very religious' would be inadequate and misleading.

7 Implications and conclusions

Five varieties of conventional religion have been described. I do not claim that these five are exhaustive of the distinguishable ways in which people in the West may be religious, and indeed I know two further types to exist. In the discussion of gnosticism we mentioned mysticism, and undoubtedly that is a distinctive type. A further type is millenarianism, the type of religiousness which is shaped by the expectation that Christ will shortly come again to judge the world. There may be more, but only the five described above emerged from the analysis of the letters to Dr Robinson. And having restricted the discussion so far to what can be established empirically, it would be foolish to embark upon speculative extensions to the typology at this point. It is possible that other types exist outside the realm of conventional religion, and that they belong to one of the forms of religion listed in the first chapter. But until further types are established in a comparable manner, we should proceed on the assumption that the five which have been described are the only types of conventional religion.

Implications for research

The findings which have been reported here have a number of implications for surveys of religion, but I shall draw out four as being particularly important.

Firstly, questionnaire items should be drawn up in the knowledge that some respondents will find them irrelevant. The most obvious illustration of this would be the exemplarist who was asked about belief in God. Now exemplarists are not anxious to advertise their atheism, and they might be unwilling to admit it except to those whom they know or trust, but questions about God are profoundly irrelevant to their way of being religious. The response, 'don't know', should therefore be treated very seriously, for it has a range of meanings, one of which is that the respondent has been asked the wrong question or a question which is without meaning. Plainly it is not possible to draw up a questionnaire in which all the items are worded to suit each of the five types described. It is not a matter of the task being complex or of the resulting questionnaire being impractically long; it is simply impossible. Phrases which have a ring of truth about them for the gnostic will, *ipso facto*, sound wrong to the theist, and the problem admits of no solution. Therefore we should recognize that respondents may want to make a guarded reply and we should make it possible for them to do so. 'Don't know', as the final item on a card which lists various possibilities, is probably one of the least satisfactory solutions to the problem, and some kind of preliminary filter question is to be preferred. One might explore the ideas of an eighteen-year-old apprentice fitter in the course of an unstructured interview and thereby discover some interesting views about the possibility of life after death, but in a questionnaire one would be wise to insert an extra item such as, 'I wonder if you have thought about whether people continue to live in some way after death?' A negative reply is respectable, regardless of whether it indicates that one has not formulated any opinion on the subject, or that one has concluded that nothing lies beyond the grave but prefers not to say so. We should not ignore the pressure which interviews put on people, or the constraints to which interviews subject them. Consider the following extract from a transcribed interview.

If you were sending in an application for a passport, and they asked you when you were born and what your name was, if one of the questions was, 'What religion are you?' what would you put in the box?
C. of E.
You'd put C. of E.?
Well, I've been to the church, so I class myself as C. of E.
But you don't go to church any more. You're not practising as a C. of E.?
No.
Then why would you put down C. of E.?
It's just a thing I've always done. I've always done that.
I was C. of E., because my family is, you know.
It's interesting. A lot of people would say just that, in fact; but

what I'm not clear in my own mind is when you're not
practising C. of E., what's the point of putting C. of E. down?
I can't really say that.
Why do you want to classify yourself as C. of E. when you're
not doing anything about it?
It's just that, you know, everyone else is putting something
down, you know. You can't put blank. They'd think you were
a right dozy person, putting black or saying I don't believe
anything, because that's not true. I do believe in something. I
believe in God, and that's what C. of E. generally is, isn't it?
Preaching about God and Jesus. And that's what I genuinely
believe in, you know. I just think about it, keep an open mind
and keep me mouth shut.[1]

We see here both the pressure exercised by the hypothetical
form, and also the pressure of the interview, leaving aside the
additional pressure the interviewer chose to exert. These
pressures are unavoidable, but they should be borne in mind in
the construction of interview schedules and questionnaires;
otherwise one analyses data which are largely artifacts of the
research instrument.

Secondly, one should not hesitate to use dichotomous
categories in eliciting responses. So-called 'strength of belief' or
'strength of commitment', are strange concepts, and to assent to
the statement, 'While I have doubts, I feel that I do believe in
God' in preference to the statement, 'I know God really exists
and I have no doubts about it', could mean any one of a variety
of things. I might mean, for example, 'I believe in God, but
probably not in the way I think your question means', in which
case my response would be wrongly interpreted as the expression
of weak belief. Simple yes/no responses are open to various
interpretations, of course, but they do not run the risk of
confusing strength of assent with the meaning of assent, and they
encourage neither-yes-nor-no responses. The need for dichotomous categories will become clearer, perhaps, if we consider
some more specific points.

So thirdly, I will suggest some suitable questions for inclusion
on a questionnaire dealing with conventional religion, and
indicate ways in which questions might be framed, in the light of
the five types of religiousness.

In asking about God, one should offer a straight yes/no choice,
but in addition present such alternatives as whether God is
regarded as awesome or familiar, whether a person or a force or
a principle. In asking about Jesus, it would seem better to ask
whether a respondent considers the life of Jesus to be of unique

significance for humanity, before asking whether he was in some sense God. As a rule, questions about the virgin birth, the resurrection, the ascension, etc., are of limited value. They indicate orthodoxy, but little more, since they are subject to so many shades of meaning. A question about the Trinity, on the other hand, is worth asking although it rarely finds a place in questionnaires. The traditionalist and the conversionist will affirm it strongly, as we have seen, and others will not feel themselves to be denying anything of great moment when they dissent. One should ask whether respondents regard human nature as fundamentally good or bad, and whether it is important to think of people as spirits or souls, or not. A number of questions can be asked about sin: does the person think that one must make a choice to turn away from sin? and do we need to be forgiven by God for some things we do? And more widely, it is important to find out whether a respondent is puzzled by evil and suffering.

The idea of salvation is central to religious views, and one should discover from what a respondent seeks to be saved, as well as by what, and for what. Attitudes to the Church, too, are significant. Do we know about God from insights which are nothing to do with religion? Should the Church be active and lively? Should it play a role in national and civic life? Traditionalism and conversionism are not easy to distinguish because they both assent to every credal formula, but conversionists are not keen to see the Church play a political role whereas traditionalists are, and conversionists insist on the need to be saved from sin, while traditionalists are more hesitant.

One should ask questions about prayer: do you pray privately? does prayer work? is it possible to heal people with prayer? can one communicate with the dead? Every questionnaire includes an item on life after death, but, as we have seen, the issue does little to discriminate between one type of religiousness and another that cannot be done more effectively in other ways. Respondents should be asked whether humanity is improving and human nature evolving, and whether, in the end, we shall be divided into the good and the bad, for these views identify the traditionalists and conversionists, and distinguish them from gnostics, with whom they share a pessimistic view of human nature. On the subject of morality it is quicker and just as efficient to ask whether God has given a set of absolute commandments than to enquire about particular moral beliefs. A question on the Bible should enable respondents to say what it is, rather than where they fall on a scale of opinions from 'literally inspired word of God' to 'edifying literature'. And, finally, information should be sought about religious groups to which a respondent belongs, for this too divides conversionists from traditionalists, the former being involved with prayer groups, bible study groups, and other devotional activities, while the latter are concerned with the Mothers' Union and the British Legion.

This is no more than a first sketch of some items which would enable a researcher to discriminate between different sorts of religiousness, and give respondents of different types a chance of being recognized as religious when otherwise they might appear to be only weakly religious.

The fourth implication for survey research is that simple analysis of marginal totals should be avoided. As we have seen, it is the combinations of responses which identify the various forms of religiousness, but these patterns occur at the level of the individual respondent, and are lost in aggregated results. Some of these patterns, indeed, cancel each other out. Ten exemplarists who say No to God and Yes to Jesus, with ten theists who say Yes to God and no to Jesus, yield twenty respondents who are all irreligious. So the cross-tabulation of results must be undertaken with the greatest care, and only after the results of other forms of multivariate analysis are known, for the findings which have been reported here would indicate that the original data matrix contains information which may too easily be lost.

Orthodox conventional religion

When talking about this study of the *Honest to God* letters, I have been asked one question repeatedly: if these five types of religiousness are so different from one another, which of them, or which combination of them, represents the 'true' Christian religion? This is not, of course, a sociological question, but it does so happen that the answer has sociological significance. The orthodox Christian tradition is made up of many different elements, and orthodoxy is defined less by prescribing a central formula than by proscribing certain tendencies in exaggerated forms. Each of the types described here exaggerates one legitimate strand in Christianity, and therein lies the clue to their relationship to one another and to normative Christianity. If all five types are taken together, and held together, they keep one another in check, and the result is 'normal' Christianity. The ideal types in fact represent no more than well know distortions. In one sense this is a disappointing conclusion to reach, but in another sense it is reassuring. Having spent much time and effort identifying the types of religiousness implicit in the data, it cannot but be a little disappointing to find that one has discovered types which are so well known that they are almost classics. One had hoped to find something new, and actually one finds only the familiar. In the end, however, this is reassuring. Five previously unknown ways of being religious would give rise to the deepest suspicion, whereas one is able to confirm, from contemporary data, that certain age-old heretical positions exercise undiminished attraction over people today. And the results are constructive, for while Gerhard Lenski can specify seven or eight 'prominent' religious orientations and select two,[2] the analysis reported here suggests that we have good reason for supposing only five to be extant, and these are five from among many more possible contenders. The sociological significance of these types proving to be well known distortions is that when ideal types are constructed from primary data they turn out to have the same properties as theoretically elaborated types. Weber insisted that an ideal type exaggerates certain aspects of a phenomenon and presents an analytically coherent account. This is what I have done in constructing the five types, but it transpires that these one-sided exaggerations existed already as distortions of a single, complex religion, and what I have done, therefore, is to add coherence. Orthodox, conventional religion, then, is composed of heresies, or ideal types, and the present task has been one of allowing them to become visible, instead of being intertwined and therefore not apparent.

The lust for certitude: a partisan view

In this final section I shall comment on one aspect of the data which has not been mentioned in the course of distinguishing types of religiousness. In the light of this comment we shall consider the types once more, and also restate the relationship of conventional religion to other sorts of religious commitment.

Uncertain – indecisive – faltering – vacillating – unsure: all are unflattering epithets, suggestive of a weak character and a lack of commitment. But there is another list of epithets which are equally disparaging: fanatical – credulous – uncompromising – intolerant – dogmatic. In considering various types of religious attitude we have seen a range of ways in which people can arrive at a sense of assurance, but it is clear that the question of certainty is always an important one. One of the strongest impressions one gains from reading the letters written to Dr Robinson is that, no matter what form it takes, the quest for religious certainty is an agonizing affair. The most striking thing revealed by the letters is the amount of anguished pain experienced by religious people. Most people, for most of the time, are thinking of quite other things, of course, but when consciously thinking about such things, and when sitting down to express their thoughts, the agony of doubt and the thirst for certainty appear. And there is no reason to suppose that what is true for these people is not equally true for others. Similarly atheists, if they are sensitive people, know the agony of doubt in respect of their atheism. Lady Katharine Russell wrote of her father, Bertrand Russell:

> I believe myself that his whole life was a search for God, or, for those who prefer less personal terms [she herself was a convert to Catholicism], for absolute certainty. Indeed he had first taken up philosophy in the hope of finding proof of the existence of God, whose childish reality had vanished before the pressing questions of his adolescent mind. He needed certainty; he loved clarity with a passion, and he could not bear any kind of muddled thinking. . . . Somewhere at the back of my father's mind, at the bottom of his heart, in the depths of his soul, there was an empty space that had once been filled by God and he never found anything else to put in it.[3]

We may, perhaps, be glad that this space remained empty, for there is reason to fear that the absolute certainty which Russell would have found acceptable would have been very similar to that of a certain Father Morris S.J. who was still alive in Russell's younger days:

> In all my life as a Catholic, now fully forty-seven years, I cannot remember a single temptation against the faith that seemed to me to have any force. The Church's teaching is before me, as a glorious series of splendid certainties. My mind is absolutely satisfied. Faith is an unmixed pleasure to me, without any pain, any difficulty, any drawback. . . . I have no private judgement to overcome, and no desire to exercise my private judgement. It is a greater pleasure to receive and possess truth with certainty, than to go in search of it and to be in uncertainty whether it has been found.[4]

In fact, however, there is no certainty, nor can there be, for it is a familiar fact of experience that the only things of which we can be certain are those which do not affect the human heart at all, while those which touch us most profoundly admit of no guarantee. The affections of others cannot be relied upon in the same way as can the services which they render to us; and yet the withdrawal of services is merely inconvenient, while withdrawal of affection is heart-breaking. We rely most on that which is intrinsically least reliable.

Certainty about things we cannot touch or see is complex, but we should note some of the implications of the manifest desire for certainty which we have observed. The cognitive style of each type of religiousness should become clearer if we focus on the need for certainty, and see the range of cognitive styles in that light. So I shall consider, first, two forms which the need for certainty commonly assumes; and then the relationship between certainty and the varities of religious belief we have seen.

One form assumed by the need for certainty results from the desire for order. There is a delicate balance between the desire for stability and the desire for change, and so Spenser's famous couplet in *The Fairie Queene:*

> Sleep after toil, port after stormy seas,
> Ease after war, death after life doth greatly please

is followed by the balancing sentiment:

> For all that moveth doth in Change delight.

Though they are opposites, novelty and stability belong together. One or the other may predominate in the values embraced by a particular person or a particular culture, but neither is tolerable without the other. There is comfort in order and there is exhilaration in change, but each is necessary and the imbalance between them does not go beyond a feeling of oppressiveness at too great an emphasis on order or a sense of alarm at change which is too sudden and catastrophic. Most of the time they exist together, alternating in a continual rhythm which we do not even notice.

There is a sense, however, in which change is natural and a stable order is not. There is nothing in our individual lives, in nature, or in human societies which is not changing all the time, and time itself would be meaningless unless it marked change. The importance of change in the religious sphere was recognized by Newman when he said that, 'To live is to change, and to be perfect is to have changed often.' The need for a secure framework nevertheless remains a pressing one, and in practice we are able to live in the flux of daily change because it follows certain predictable patterns. We are used to living in an orderly world: buses come roughly on time or we should not wait for them; food stops that rumbling in the stomach or we should not look forward to meal times as much as we do; the news is read at 8 o'clock each morning, prompt, and if it were otherwise we should be less precise about the time when we switch on the radio. Our dependence on order becomes apparent when life is thrown into chaos, as, for example, when the electricity supply is switched off, and it would be extremely unnerving if, from time to time, it went off for anything from half an hour to three weeks without warning. Fortunately these things are under our control or under the control of someone we can trust, and even the weather, which we cannot control, does not take us completely by surprise, for although we may not get sunshine to order it does at least follow a more or less orderly pattern and we are warned when the pattern is going to be disrupted. But accidents still happen and they can be unnerving just because they are unexpected. Science is not yet perfect, and medical science in particular is far from being able to prepare us for pain, madness or death, and much less able to prevent these unpleasant surprises.

So even in a scientific culture like that of the West it is possible for an orderly life to break down. Runaway inflation, or the rapid decline of the cotton industry, can affect the lives of great numbers of people, and as individuals we are even more vulnerable: the shocks of redundancy, of failing an examination, or of bereavement profoundly distress people every day. For reasons which are obvious, the working class are more at risk than are those whose wealth gives them power and control over more aspects of their lives, either directly, or indirectly through education and access to a variety of services.

As long as serious disorder continues regularly to break through the orderliness of life, people will tend to concoct some scheme whereby they are able to place the unforeseen within the context of a larger order. The explanation which people invoke today will draw on the remembered explanation to which an earlier generation appealed when confronted with some comparable rupture in the routine of life, and when the present trauma has passed and equanimity returns, the explanation is not entirely forgotten, but is stored away and carefully cherished against the next time disaster strikes. In asserting the truth of an explanation at times when it is not needed, people are, as it were, paying their insurance premiums against the day when a claim is made; the higher the premium you pay, the more fully you are covered when the rainy day comes; and the more claims you make, the higher will be the premium. So the nervous and accident-prone are ideal targets for the insurance salesman, as are those who have just had an accident.

When disorder causes anxiety and distress to people in western culture, there are three options open to them, although the choice will exist only in the eyes of a bystander. The initial response is one of shock, leaving the person unable to act, perhaps numb and devoid of feelings. After the initial shock, however, either (a) they may suffer the distress and recover as best they may, waiting for the confusion to pass and for an orderly pattern to reassert itself. It may not, of course, and there is always the possibility that someone will remain disorientated, unable ever again to feel a stability and equilibrium within which to live an ordered life. Or (b) that which is distressing is placed in a wider context of order which includes the supernatural. If people already have a conviction that some wider order exists it may be invoked in such situations, and the disorderly character of the situation is thus transformed so that the disorder appears to have been only superficial. The concept of Providence, for example, can encompass everything, although this Providence may not normally be thought of as being especially active. Or (c) in situations of distress, belief in some supernatural order may command the credence of people for the first time. No doubt psychological mechanisms connected with a state of shock make people more suggestible and more credulous at such times, but a disordered situation will in any case evoke the need to rediscover order, even in one who can remain cool and composed. Disorderly, unpredictable and chance events are abhorrent to human nature. What we can control, we control; what we cannot control we seek to predict; what defies our powers of prediction we accept as random events which still obey the laws of probability: but order is never absent. There is nothing which does not follow the orders of someone or something, either the laws which are imposed upon it or the laws which it imposes upon itself. The orderliness is an essential part of the way in which we perceive the world, and it is certainly not just the fad of a few tidy-minded individuals.

One of the most striking features of the supernatural is that it introduces more order than there would be without it. It extends the range and scope of the orderly world; it brings within the framework of an orderly pattern events which otherwise would appear capricious; and it gives an added sureness and certainty to whatever is regular. A religious view – a view, that is, which perceives and values elements of reality beyond the natural realm – sees a world which is more orderly, and more surely ordered, than the world which is seen by the eye unaided by such a view.

People feel secure to the extent that there is order and regularity in their surroundings. It is because they find it so difficult to live with uncertainty and insecurity that they have subjected themselves to political regimes which severely curtail their freedom. They do not accept discipline and authority because it is the most effective way of making a better world, but because it is more comfortable, like a return to childhood dependence in which one is free of the burden of freedom. The same thing which makes an authoritarian political regime attractive to some serves to commend a religious view to others, for it too removes doubt by imposing order. No two types of religious attitude promise the same order, of course, and none is compatible with the others, but that serves to highlight further the way in which religion is characterized by its orderliness. It is not this or that particular order which characterizes it, but order in general.

The experience of disorder is disquieting and unsettling because we feel ourselves threatened by a chaos in which we are unable to act: the world seems no longer to fit together in a way we understand and we are frightened of doing anything at all lest we do the wrong thing. A bathroom in which the light switch flushed the lavatory and the bath taps operated an electric razor would be unnerving, and the person who was unperturbed by such unpredictability would be less a human being than a machine; if one retained total equanimity one would be successfully conducting experiments rather than living a human life. Paradoxically, however, the machine, which alone is capable of surviving in complete disorder, is also alone in being able to tolerate a totally ordered world. You would have to be an automaton if you were to keep your sanity either in Alice's Wonderland or in Aldous Huxley's Brave New World. Human nature seems to demand that there be a basic degree of both stability and novelty in the world, and the need for order is powerfully expressed and potently reinforced by the need for religious certainty, which is order on a cosmic scale.

A second form which is assumed by the need for certainty is shaped by the desire to find meaning in the world. The search for meaning is not an alternative to the search for order, since the very existence of order poses for some people the question of its meaning. For other people, however, it is particular events which fall outside an established order which seem to demand that they be given meaning. Unique events demand particular explanations, but even the ordered patterning of many events is a unique event which may seem to demand explanation.

Whenever we say of something which has happened that we 'have to make sense' of it, we grope for an explanation. The occasions of such gropings are manifold. Experiences of beauty and of barbarity, of order and of chaos, of love and of hatred, and of many other things besides, are hard for some people to accept as merely happening to be that way, for they seem to embody some purpose whether for good or for ill. Some people believe that beauty is in the eye of the beholder, but for other people that account fails to do justice to their experience, and even to violate it; they say of a scene that its beauty is so manifest and incontestable that it compels their wonder and admiration, and that it confronts them as an objective fact which requires some further explanation. Or again a man may look back at his life when a good part of it is spent and, reflecting on it, detect in the mosaic of failures and successes, of virtues and vices, of good and bad fortune, some sort of pattern which enables him to recognize that, in some sense, it all seems to hang together – he may even be able to say that it seems 'meant' to have happened that way. As a rule, religion meets this need to find meaning by asserting that there is indeed a purpose at work in the inscrutable will of an all-powerful God. Another form of religion, as we have seen, may discern a purpose at work which it cannot deny and yet which it is unable to attribute to any personal Will. The experience of a need to find meaning is potentially, however, a religious experience, for it is the opposite of the view that beauty is in the eye of the beholder. When people are confronted by the recognition of a meaning or a purpose in life, be it manifest or mysterious, they feel that it must originate from outside themselves, from that which transcends them.

Both the search for order and the search for meaning may lead to a religious view being held with certainty. It may be that the extent to which certainty is claimed for religious beliefs depends upon the extent to which a person needs order or certainty, for reasons of temperament or circumstance. Neither need lead to this end, however, and so we must distinguish between religious knowledge as it occurs normally, and religious knowledge marked by certainty. For this purpose let us admit the word faith, and use it as a generic term for the manner in which a religious view is held. Now faith is not the same as doubt, but it is clearly different from certainty. To have faith in someone or something suggests trust, confidence, reliance, and when one acts in good faith one expects to be trusted. Generically, this is the characteristic cognitive style of conventional religion, and it includes the hope of exemplarism and the trust of theism. By contrast, the assurance of conversionism and the knowledge of gnosticism enjoy certitude, i.e. the feeling of certainty, but what they gain in certitude they lose in faith, for the two attitudes of mind are mutually exclusive. The search for order or for meaning can lead either to faith, or beyond it, to certitude. If faith is less sure than certitude, it more than makes up for this lack of sureness by being aware of the inherently complex and problematical character of the events or experiences demanding explanation, and thus it is a more sensitive form of knowledge. Ignorance and certitude are both inert in the search for knowledge, for the one has not set out on the quest, while the other believes itself to have arrived, and neither therefore allows for the possibility of further discovery. We may say that faith is three-quarters of the way along the road which leads to certitude, but that the road is one which rises slowly to a high summit of faith whence the traveller can see the country spread out ahead clearly, but in all its complexity; thereafter the road drops steeply into certitude, and having arrived there the final destination is seen only partially, from very close quarters and from one angle. Those who set out on the quest for religious knowledge often have trouble in not overshooting the summit, but when they do overshoot it and descend into certitude, their last state is no better than their first, despite the fact that they are on the other side of the hill. In common with our own day, the Victorian era was particularly notable for overshooting the summit and Disraeli's judgment on the belief of his own times was clear: 'I hold that the characteristic of the present age is craving credulity.'

Certitude occurs in two distinct guises: as a fact and as a need. Certitude as a fact is certainty which is assumed and taken for granted. In our culture it is the empirical findings of established science which most obviously command certitude. No-one argues about whether the earth is roughly spherical or whether the sun truly is 93 million miles away, for the truth of those propositions is never questioned let alone discussed. We bestow certitude upon these beliefs because we deem them true, but the certitude itself, i.e. our subjective feeling of certainty, is a fact which cannot be wished out of existence. If, *per impossibile*, it were shown a century hence that both beliefs are incorrect and that the earth's shape is paraboloid and the sun 10 light years away, that would have a bearing on the truth of today's beliefs, but it would not affect the fact of today's certainty about them.

Certitude as a need, on the other hand, is altogether different. Nazi Germany wished its citizens to believe that 'Aryans' were intrinsically superior to 'non-Aryans', and the Republic of South Africa today maintains that whites are superior to blacks, and in each case the response of unquestioning belief is expected. Now the truth or falsity of these propositions is irrelevant for our purposes; what is important is that they are not the certainties they are proclaimed to be. Even if argument and debate about their truth is silenced so effectively that no dissenting voice is heard, the very frequency with which the propositions are asserted and reasserted, and the many aruguments which are rehearsed to demonstrate their truth, show that the certainty which is wished for has not been attained, or there would be no need for persuasion. The constant assertions force one to conclude that the lady doth protest too much. The absence of discussion about a belief and the silent assumption of its truth show that it is held with certitude; repeated vociferous assertions, on the other hand, demonstrate that a need for certitude exists. The truth or falsity of particular beliefs is not at issue, but only the nature of the certitude with which they are held. To recapitulate, we can distinguish two aspects of certitude, or the feeling of certainty:

Certitude is the absence of doubt.
The need for certitude is the attempt to escape from doubt.

In the light of this distinction, and of the characterizations of the two forms of certitude, it will be clear, I think, that in religious matters in our own generation we encounter the need for certitude, not simple certitude, and the pain which is so obvious in the letters to Dr Robinson speaks eloquently of that need.

I have asserted that faith is the characteristic cognitive style of conventional religion, and that it is superior to certitude. In making the latter assertion I have ventured a judgment which oversteps the bounds of social science. I believe it is a reasonable judgment, however, and I shall explain it a little further. Faith as a cognitive style implies a continuous act of aspiration, not an act of attainment. It is concerned with a vision of the truth which has constantly to be reviewed, renewed, striven towards, and held on to; the vision is never beyond doubt and never firmly in one's grasp, for if it were it would have ceased to be a vision and it would have ceased to be faith. Doubt, in other words, is an intrinsic part of faith, and since certitude is marked by the absence of doubt, or the attempt to escape from it, this places the two in sharp contrast. Certitude overshoots faith, craving for sureness. Instead of having a vision it makes a blueprint, and by fleeing from the last vestige of uncertainty it ceases to be conventionally religious, becoming religious in a degenerate sense. The superiority of faith to certitude is obvious. Religion concerns the transcendent or suprahuman, and religious knowledge can therefore never be marked by the certainty of knowledge derived from the human senses; conversely, if one knows something with complete certainty, then, by definition, what is thus certainly known cannot be transcendent. That which is beyond one can only be aspired to and reached towards, never grasped. Certitude is a stunted growth compared with faith, which is as large as the human heart and mind can imagine – and larger, because it always strains at the leash of nature, aspiring to that which, if it exists at all, is beyond.

Having identified the characteristic cognitive style of conventional religion we are in a position to see more clearly the ways in which it differs from the other kinds of religion which were mentioned in the first chapter.

Sectarian religion is different because its characteristic is the need for certitude, not faith. Conversionism and gnosticism are styles of conventional religion which are 'degenerate' precisely because they are incipiently sectarian, and it is no accident that they appear as fully developed styles of religion outside the domain of conventional religion in sectarian form.

New religious movements, too, are different. In some cases they are purely experimental forms of commitment which do not require faith. In other cases they are like the more intense sects and require more, in the shape of certitude.

Popular religion, like primitive religion, is different, because its cognitive style is one of certitude, not faith or the need for certitude. Cognitively as well as historically, it is pre-religious by comparison with conventional religion.

Surrogate religion is different, but the difference goes beyond disparities of cognitive styles. The example most often cited is communism in the USSR, and it can be seen as distinct because it is concerned with the transcendent only in the sense of those things which transcend individual human experience in a natural and temporal sense.

Invisible religion is distinct from conventional religion for the same reason, but its cognitive style is characteristically different too. As a category in the Durkheimian tradition, it is not surprising that the themes of invisible religion, although selected in the private rather than the public sphere, are experienced as having an obligatory character. As such, the belief in self-realization, for example, is a matter of certitude, not faith.

Civil religion stands on its own. It would be possible to argue that American civil religion comes closer to being conventionally religious than does the religion found in the Churches and denominations in the USA. It entails faith rather than certitude, and its invocation of God marks its transcendent character. In a culture which speaks naturally of 'religious preference' rather than religious commitment, civil religion is the conventional religion, while the Moral Majority stands as its degraded, sectarian form.

I have attempted here to put conventional or official religion back into the limelight. Recent work in the sociology of religion has tended to pass on to what appear more interesting topics, such as new religious movements and modern meaning systems. My argument is that we have yet to give an adequate sociological account of conventional religion, and that if we were to succeed in doing so we should be better equipped for the study of those remoter topics. We have much more to learn about conventional religion before we can regard it as being sufficiently studied and adequately understood.

Notes

Chapter 1 Varieties of religion

1 For an analysis of Durkheim's position, see S. Lukes, *Emile Durkheim*, London, Allen Lane, 1973, pp. 474-7.

2 This perspective has been crudely empirical in comparison with Weber's own work and has been influenced as much if not more by the British survey tradition and the practices of market research, but it is to Weber that it looks for theoretical legitimation rather than to Marx.

3 T. Luckmann, *The Invisible Religion*, London, Collier–Macmillan, 1967. The work appeared in a German edition in 1963, but, as the author tells us in his Foreword, it originated as a review, published in 1960, which was prompted by his 'dissatisfaction with the limitations of various empirical studies in the sociology of religion', and more immediately as an unpublished essay entitled, 'Notes on the Case of the Missing Religion', all of which is interesting background information in the light of subsequent developments.

4 Contribution to F. Abauzit et al., *Le Sentiment religieux à l'heure actuelle*, Paris, Vrin, 1919, quoted in Lukes, op. cit., p. 516.

5 Luckmann, op. cit., pp. 90-1.

6 Ibid., p. 102.

7 The element of *bricolage* in Luckmann's model has not been taken up, however, and the tendency has been to identify a small number of pre-selected packages from which people choose. The reason for this may be practical rather than theoretical, since sociologists show a marked disinclination to allow for individual differences when they are looking for socially significant patterns. This is a point to which we shall return.

8 B.R. Wilson, 'An analysis of sect development', reprinted in Wilson (ed.), *Patterns of Sectarianism*, London, Heinemann, 1967, p. 24; Wilson's classic article still gives the clearest account of the distinction between the religion of the churches and dominations and that of the sects.

9 In this respect certain new religious movements are more like sects in Eastern religions, where the characterization of sects used here is inappropriate.

10 This is the most usual name and it is particularly useful in distinguishing the formal and systematic religion of religious specialists and cultural elites in the East from the religion of the masses. For a recent set of essays, see P.H. Vrijhof and J. Waardenburg (eds), *Official and Popular Religion*, The Hague, Mouton, 1979.

11 A term used in contradistinction to 'universal religion' in much the same way as popular/official; see G. Mensching, 'Folk religion and universal religion', trans. L. Schneider (ed.) *Religion, Culture and Society*, New York, Wiley, 1964.

12 R.C. Towler, *Homo Religiosus*, London, Constable, 1974, Chap. 8.

13 D.A. Martin, *A Sociology of English Religion*, London, SCM Press, 1967, pp. 74-6 and 114-15.

14 R.N. Bellah, 'Civil religion in America', reprinted in Bellah, *Beyond Belief*, New York, Harper & Row, 1970, pp. 169-89, and also *The Broken Covenant: American Civil Religion in Time of Trial*, New York, Seabury Press, 1975.

15 R. Robertson, *The Sociological Interpretation of Religion*, Oxford, Blackwell, 1970, pp. 39 ff.

16 E.I. Bailey, 'Emergent mandalas: the implicit religion of contemporary society', unpublished Ph.D. thesis, University of Bristol, 1976.

17 J. Goody, 'Religion and ritual: the definitional problem', *British Journal of Sociology*, vol. 12, 1961, pp. 142-64, was one of the earlier defences of 'exclusive' definitions in the face of 'inclusive' ones; for a discussion of the debate, see Robertson, op. cit., pp. 34-51.

18 Luckmann, op. cit., p. 107.

19 R. Wuthnow, *The Consciousness Reformation*, Berkeley, University of California Press, 1976. In the course of subsequent debate Wuthnow has defined a meaning system as:

> the dominant meanings in a culture that are associated with a particular set of symbols. Its distinguishing feature is an identifiable set of *symbols* with which interpretations, feelings, and activities can be associated. A world-view or belief system, in contrast, consists of all the *beliefs* that an individual holds about the nature of reality. An individual's world-view can thus be comprised of beliefs about any number of symbols, but a meaning system, by comparison, pertains to one set of symbols, even though these symbols may be used in a number of different texts, settings, or collectivities. (Wuthnow, 'Two traditions in the study of religion, *Journal for the Scientific Study of Religion*, vol. 20, 1981, p. 24.)

20 Wuthnow, 'Two traditions', op. cit., p.25.

21 Ibid.

22 Wuthnow, *The Consciousness Reformation*, op. cit., p.3.

23 R. Stark and W.S. Bainbridge, 'Towards a theory of religion:

religious commitment', *Journal for the Scientific Study of Religion*, vol. 19, 1980, pp. 114-28.

24 W.S. Bainbridge and R. Stark, 'The "Consciousness Reformation" reconsidered', *Journal for the Scientific Study of Religion*, vol. 20, 1981, p.4.

25 Ibid., p. 2.

26 R. Stark, 'Must all religion be supernatural?' in B.R. Wilson (ed.) *The Social Impact of New Religious Movements*, New York, Rose of Sharon Press, 1981.

27 R. Stark and W.S. Bainbridge, 'Secularization and cult formation in the Jazz Age', *Journal for the Scientific Study of Religion*, vol. 20, 1981, pp. 360-73.

28 One would expect 'Theism' items to behave in the way they report, and to be shared in the way they report, because they are indicators of 'being religious' in the conventional and readily communicated way. They are well known slogans for religion in the way that, in Britain, well known slogans exist for 'being Labour' and for 'being Tory'. On the problem of 'general religiousness', see Towler, op. cit., pp. 145-6. Stark's view is expressed thus:

> I maintain that there can be no wholly naturalistic religion: a religion lacking supernatural assumptions is no religion at all . . . the differences between supernatural and non-supernatural systems are so profound that it makes no more sense to equate them than to equate totem poles and telegraph poles. (Stark, op. cit., p. 159.)

29 W.C. McCready with A.M. Greeley, *The Ultimate Values of the American Population*, Beverley Hills, Sage, 1976, p. 6.

30 Ibid., p. 18.

31 Ibid., p. 19; for later work they collapsed numbers 2 and 3 into 'secular optimist', and numbers 5 and 6 into 'hopeful', adding a new fifth category, 'diffuse'.

32 Ibid., p. 197; the run-in was:

> 'Now I am going to describe some situations to you. These are things that happen to people sometimes, and I want you to *imagine* that they are happening to you. Please tell me which response in the card comes closest to your own feelings.' (Ibid.)

33 P.L. Berger and T. Luckmann, *The Social Construction of Reality*, London, Allen Lane, 1967. Of this they write:

> The concept of reality structuring or the construction of reality is known to us because it has been dealt with theoretically. This theoretical work, however, has been carried out at a high level of generality, and it has not informed empirical research on contemporary social life. (C.Y. Glock and T. Piazza, 'Exploring reality structures' in T. Robbins and D. Anthony (eds), *In Gods We Trust: New Patterns of Religious Pluralism in America*, New York, Transaction Books, 1981 – first appeared in *Society*, vol. 15, no. 4 (May/June), 1978.)

34 Glock and Piazza, op. cit., p. 68.
35 Bainbridge and Stark, 'The "Consciousness Reformation" reconsidered', op. cit., p. 1; cf. Towler, op. cit., pp. 152-4.
36 Wuthnow, 'Two traditions in the study of religion', op. cit., p. 27.
37 L. Schneider and S. Dornbusch, *Popular Religion: Inspirational Books in America*, Chicago, University of Chicago Press, 1958.
38 W.I. Thomas and F. Znaniecki, *The Polish Peasant in Europe and America*, New York, Knopf, 1927.
39 C.Y. Glock and R. Stark, *Religion and Society in Tension*, Chicago, Rand McNally, 1965.
40 Ibid., pp. 24-5.
41 Ibid., p. 90; this is in contrast to the repeated Gallup findings that 96 to 97 per cent of Americans say 'Yes' in answer to the question, 'Do you believe in God?'
42 Ibid., Table 5-1, p. 91; the highest figure for 'higher power' is for Congregationalists among the Protestants.
43 G. Lenski, *The Religious Factor: A Sociological Study of Religion's Impact on Politics, Economics and Family Life*, revised edn, Garden City, New York, Doubleday Anchor Books, 1963.
44 Ibid., p. 18.
45 Ibid., pp. 24-5; Lenski notes that 'associational involvement' may be thought of as a measure of a 'collectivist orientation'. Glock and Stark refer to these two, two-fold measures as 'four indicators of religiosity' (op. cit., p. 22), but Lenski remarks that, 'orthodoxy and devotionalism are not merely two alternative measures of "religiosity" as is so often imagined. On the contrary, they are separate and independent orientations, and each has its own peculiar consequences for the behaviour of individuals'. (p. 26)
46 Together with research colleagues, I recently conducted such a survey, with the support of an SSRC research grant, 'Conventional religion and common religion in Leeds: a case study', which studied a random sample of 2000 adults.
47 See p. 76 below, and note 8 to Chap. 5.
48 It is not difficult to find letters from working-class people, who write to radio and television stations, for example, but young working-class males are not great letter-writers and they pose a greater problem.
49 Cf. note 19 above.
50 M. Weber, *The Methodology of the Social Sciences*, trans. E.A. Shils and H.A. Finch, New York, Free Press, 1949, pp. 89 ff.
51 Quoted in Lukes, op. cit., p. 515.

Chapter 2   Exemplarism

1 Max Weber, *The Sociology of Religion*, Boston, Beacon Press, 1963, Chap. 4 *passim* (first German edition 1922); Weber prefers the term 'emissary' to 'ethical' prophet.
2 The most useful general account is, perhaps, John Knox, *The Humanity and Divinity of Christ*, Cambridge, Cambridge University Press, 1967.

3 F.L. Cross (ed.) *The Oxford Dictionary of the Christian Church*, London, Oxford University Press, 1957, q.v. Abelard.

4 Owen Chadwick, *The Secularization of the European Mind in the Nineteenth Century*, Cambridge, Cambridge University Press, 1975, p. 219.

5 Ibid., p. 220.

6 Renan, quoted in ibid.

7 Quoted in ibid, p. 216.

8 For a readable account of Modernism, see Alec Vidler, *A Variety of Catholic Modernists*, Cambridge, Cambridge University Press, 1970.

9 This development is the theme explored in Peter L. Berger, *The Heretical Imperative*, London, Collins, 1980.

10 Don Cupitt, *Taking Leave of God*, London, SCM Press, 1980.

11 Lionel Trilling, *Sincerity and Authenticity*, London, Oxford University Press, 1972.

12 Richard Sennett, *The Fall of Public Man*, Cambridge, Cambridge University Press, 1977.

13 Richard Hoggart, *The Uses of Literacy*, Harmondsworth, Penguin, 1958, p. 117.

14 Ibid., pp. 117-19.

15 For the differentiation of religious institutions, see Thomas Luckmann, *The Invisible Religion*, London, Collier-Macmillan, 1967, pp. 61-8.

16 William Temple is reputed to have said that the Church is the only organization which exists for the sake of those outside it, which may perhaps be taken as an example of a prophetic truth as opposed to an empirical truth.

17 The expression, 'cognitive style', is used here in a way somewhat different from that in which it is used by either Schutz or Heidegger; see, e.g. Alfred Schutz and Thomas Luckmann, *The Structures of the Life-World*, London, Heinemann, 1974, Chap. 2, Sec. [A]2 'The style of lived experience: namely, the cognitive style and the tension of consciousness'. To compare the distinctions which are drawn by the various usages of the expression would be a complex but rewarding exercise.

18 Rodney Needham, *Belief, Language, and Experience*, Oxford, Blackwell, 1972, p. 188, emphasis added; Needham attributes the phrase, 'tone of thought', to Friedrich Waismann (*How I See Philosophy*, edited by R. Harré, London, Macmillan, 1968, p. 65).

19 Someone who was brought up a devoutly religious Jew, became a Marxist atheist, and finally joined the Divine Light Mission would, if my contention is sound, be personally aware of three very different meanings of 'belief'.

20 I am indebted to my colleague Zygmunt Bauman for drawing this point to my attention, and it is one to which I have alluded already on pp. 21f above. I have discussed the relevance of a Durkheimian perspective to this issue in chapter 4 of an earlier book, *Homo Religiosus*, London, Constable, 1974.

21 This is not, of course, to say that religion and religious movements

have lost such power, and refers solely to the case of exemplarism.

22 The Samaritans were started in the City of London by the Reverend Chad Varah in 1953. There are now 170 branches, staffed by 20,000 volunteers, offering 'a free and completely confidential befriending service'.

23 Such might be the view of Edward Norman, the BBC Reith Lecturer for 1978 (E.R. Norman, *Christianity and the World Order*, Oxford, Oxford University Press, 1979).

Chapter 3   Conversionism

1 William Temple, *Readings in St John's Gospel*, London, Macmillan, 1945, p. 24.

2 Article IX among the Thirty-Nine Articles of Religion of the Church of England.

3 Robert Towler and A.P.M. Coxon, *The Fate of the Anglican Clergy*, London, Macmillan, 1979, pp. 165-6.

4 See, for example, David Hay, *Exploring Inner Space*, Harmondsworth, Penguin, 1982.

5 William James, *The Varieties of Religious Experience* (Gifford Lectures for 1901-2), London, Collins, 1960, p. 257, emphasis added.

6 My father, who, like his father and grandfather before him, was a barber, went one day to shave a man of very advanced years. The old gentleman, who had been a life-long Salvationist, was looked after by his daughter, who announced by father's arrival by saying, 'Mr Towler's here, Father: he's come to shave you,' which received the puzzled reply, 'He can't do that: I've been saved these eighty years.'

7 Max Weber's remarks about the Church and the Sect, though of great value in their context, need to be modified if they are to aid an understanding of religiosity more than fifty years after his death. Weber did not, of course, refer to a distinction between 'high' and 'low' doctrines of the Church (Max Weber, Introductory essay to 'The Economic Ethic of the World Religions', translated under the title, 'The Social Psychology of the World Religions' in H.H. Gerth and C. Wright Mills, *From Max Weber*, London, Routledge & Kegan Paul, 1948).

8 A valuable aid to the general understanding of contemporary religiosity is Bernice Martin, *A Sociology of Contemporary Cultural Change*, Oxford, Blackwell, 1981.

9 People generally speak of 'being converted to' Roman Catholicism or of 'submitting to the claims of Rome', which, while passive, does not imply personal passivity. The striking contrast is with becoming Jewish, where the verb is stridently in the active mood, and the sentence usually ungrammatical: 'He is going to convert.' But Judaism is not a proselytizing religion.

10 Cf. Weber:

It is quite understandable that the more weighty the civic strata as such have been, the more they have been torn from bonds of taboo and from division into sibs and castes, and the more favourable has been the soil for religions that call for action in this world. Under these conditions the preferred religious attitude could become the attitude of active asceticism, of God-willed action nourished by *the sentiment of being God's tool*, rather than the possession of the deity or the inward and contemplative surrender to God, which has appeared as the supreme value to religions influenced by strata of genteel intellectuals. (Op. cit., p. 285.)

11 Typically they do not, which is not to say that it never happens.
12 Emile Durkheim, *The Elementary Forms of the Religious Life*, trans. J. W. Swain (2nd edn), London, George Allen & Unwin, 1976, p. 220.
13 Conversionists will defend the sexual division of labour as 'natural' although it is (as far as I know) without scriptural warrant.
14 See Weber's essay, 'Religious Rejections of the World and their Directions', Gerth and Wright Mills, op. cit., pp. 323-59, especially pp. 340f.; a classic study is H. Richard Niebuhr, *Christ Against Culture*, New York, Harper, 1951, where his discussion of Tolstoy is particularly instructive for an understanding of conversionism.
15 The rise of 'creationist' thinking is interesting, and it should be noted that it is not a characteristic element of conversionism as described here. For religion and science in general, see Eileen Barker, 'Science as theology: the theological functioning of western science', in M. Hesse and A. Peacocke (eds), *Sciences and Theology in the 20th Century*, Boston, Oriel Press, 1981.

Chapter 4   Theism

1 The review, published in the *Observer* (24 March 1963), was a response to Dr Robinson's article in the same paper the week before, summing up the argument of *Honest to God* under the headline, 'OUR IMAGE OF GOD MUST GO'.
2 Just as, inversely, theories of primitive religion often turn out to be primitive theories of religion, as Evans-Pritchard pointed out.
3 V.W. Turner, *The Ritual Process*, London, Routledge & Kegan Paul, 1969; the level of analysis involved is quite different, of course, as is the level of Turner's concepts as he develops them compared with their origins at the level of the analysis of rites, following Arnold van Gennep (*The Rites of Passage*, London, Routledge & Kegan Paul, 1960).
4 Hoggart, *The Uses of Literacy*, Harmondsworth, Penguin, 1958, p. 164.
5 Thus the *Concise Oxford Dictionary* entry for 'belief' begins: 'Trust or confidence (*in*)'; for a full discussion, see Needham, *Belief, Language and Experience*, Oxford, Blackwell, 1972, Chap. 4.

Chapter 5   Gnosticism

1 The name is chosen in conformity with the usage established by

Bryan Wilson ('An analysis of sect development', reprinted in Wilson (ed.), *Patterns of Sectarianism*, London, Heinemann, 1967).

2 See Weber, 'Religious Rejections of the World and their Directions' in H.H. Gerth and C. Wright Mills, *From Max Weber*, London, Routledge & Kegan Paul, 1948, p. 358; only dualism, predestination, and kharma are seen by Weber as rationally consistent, which does not necessarily mean that they are viable, as his remarks about the Parsees indicate.

3 Of Gnostic doctrines at the time of the early Christian Church, *The Oxford Dictionary of the Christian Church* says:

> Characteristic of Gnostic teaching was the distinction between the Demiurge or 'creator god' and the supreme, remote and unknowable Divine Being. From the latter the Demiurge was derived by a longer or shorter series of emanations or 'aeons'. He it was who, through some mischance or fall among the higher aeons, was the immediate source of creation and ruled the world, which was therefore imperfect and antagonistic to what was truly spiritual. But into the constitution of some men there had entered a seed or spark of Divine spiritual substance, and through 'gnosis' and the rites associated with it the spiritual element might be rescued from its evil material environment and assured of a return to its home in the Divine Being. Such men were designated the 'spiritual', while others were merely 'fleshly' or 'material', though some Gnostics added a third intermediate class, the 'psychic'. The function of Christ was to come as the emissary of the supreme God, bringing 'gnosis'. As a Divine Being He neither assumed a properly human body nor died, but either temporarily inhabited a human being, Jesus, or assumed a merely phantasmal human appearance.

4 Conversionism, by contrast, was immediately obvious, particularly in the form of evangelical fundamentalism, and letters containing that type of religiousness were numerous.

5 Since the analysis was not quantitative this statement reflects an impression rather than an observation.

6 Thus St Teresa of Avila wrote of certain perceptions of the spiritual world:

> I most earnestly advise you, when you hear or know of God's bestowing these graces on others, never to pray or desire to be led by this way yourself though it may appear to you to be very good.

And of the effects on the 'soul' of having arrived at the mystical knowledge of God, she says that the first is,

> a self-forgetfulness so complete that she seems not to exist, for such a transformation has been worked in her that she no longer recognizes herself; nor does she remember that heaven, or life or glory are to be hers, for she is entirely occupied in striving to glorify God. (*The Interior Castle or The Mansions*, trans. by a

117

Benedictine of Stanbrook, abridged and edited by H. Martin, London, SCM Press, 1958, pp. 108 and 119.)

7 In its modern form, Spiritualism dates from the occult experiences of the Fox family in America in 1848, but the ideas have a continuous history in the Judaeo-Christian tradition from the earliest story of necromancy in I Samuel xxviii.8, from which it would appear that the beliefs and practices were fully institutionalized by the time of David (c. tenth century BC). For modern Spiritualism, see G. K. Nelson, *Spiritualism and Society*, London, Routledge & Kegan Paul, 1969.

8 The letter, which is complete, also illustrates the way in which many people who wrote to Dr Robinson did so simply to express their own views and without reference to the *Honest to God* debate (see pp. 15-16 above).

Chapter 6 Traditionalism

1 For a discussion of the definitions Durkheim employed, see S. Lukes, *Emile Durkheim*, London, Allen Lane, 1973, Chaps. 11 and 23.

2 'Individualism and the intellectuals', trans. S. and J. Lukes, reprinted in W.S.F. Pickering, *Durkheim on Religion*, London, Routledge & Kegan Paul, 1975, p. 66.

3 For other modern ideas which Durkheim saw as in some sense, sacred, see *The Elementary Forms of the Religious Life*, trans. J. W. Swain (2nd edn), London, George Allen & Unwin, 1976, pp. 214-16.

4 Thomas Luckmann, *The Invisible Religion*, London, Collier-Macmillan, 1967, Chapter 7.

5 Tracing back the etymology of 'belief', Needham finds, 'to hold dear, cherish, trust in' to be the meaning of the root word in Common Germanic (*Belief, Language and Experience*, Oxford, Blackwell, 1972, p. 41).

6 Furthermore, once the tradition has ceased to be traditional, it can never again become a viable option. The point was made by the medieval Muslim philosopher, Al Ghazali: 'There is no hope of returning to a traditional faith after it has once been abandoned, since the essential condition in the holder of a traditional faith is that he should not know he is a traditionalist.' (Quoted in E. Gellner, *Legitimation of Belief*, London, Cambridge University Press, 1974.)

7 There is an argument that rites are dysfunctional, on the grounds that a rite may provoke anxieties and questions which would not have occurred without it. The counter-argument is that this does not matter, since the rite can allay the anxieties it arouses and answer the questions to which it gives rise, and that the net result will be positive since the event will have been marked more forcibly as a result of the anxiety, etc.

8 There is a pleasing irony in the fact that the most vocal support for tradition commonly comes from those who do not rely on it. Thus it was Marghanita Laski who led the protests about Choral Evensong's move from the BBC's Home Service, and David Martin who organized opposition to the Church of England's Alternative Services

Book, neither of whom is a traditionalist by any stretch of the imagination.

9 Peter L. Berger, 'A sociological view of the secularization of theology', *Journal for the Scientific Study of Religion*, vol. 6, 1967, p. 15.

10 Dr Robinson had appeared as a witness for the defence in the case brought against the publishers of *Lady Chatterley's Lover*.

Chapter 7 Implications and conclusions

1 Bernice Martin and Ronald Pluck, *Young People's Beliefs*, unpublished report to the Board of Education, General Synod of the Church of England, 1976.

2 See p. 14 above.

3 Katharine Tait, *My Father, Bertrand Russell*, quoted in Maurice Cranston, 'Bertrand Russell: towards a complete portrait', *Encounter*, April 1976, p. 68.

4 M.D. Petre, *Autobiography and Life of George Tyrrell*, 2 vols. London, Edward Arnold, 1912, vol. I, p. 258.

Appendix
Catalogue of themes in *Honest to God* letters (7th draft, 10 December 1974)

Reactions to HTG

1.1.1.1	What do you mean? (823)
1.1.1.2	Please define your terms/words (1)
1.1.2.1	Re-write in simple language please (2689, 1119, 1904)
1.1.2.2	You have been misunderstood (2909)
1.2	Agreement (1483)
1.3.1	You say what we feel but can't express (2909)
1.3.2	Relief at no longer having to believe x (2423)
1.3.3	You've relieved my sense of guilt (2561, 1784)
1.3.4	You've relieved my sense of isolation; Intellectual empathy (1280)
1.3.5	You've given us the courage to be honest in our beliefs (209, 3178, 694)
1.3.6	You've stimulated thought and discussion (306)
1.3.7	I find your work interesting (1565)
1.3.8	You've helped to clarify/form my/our thoughts/ideas (1104)
1.4.1	You, as a member of the Church establishment, have given us hope. You make it possible to go on looking for a new formulation (1895)
1.4.2	I'm troubled: please help me (2704)
1.4.3	Bishops have no right to be unorthodox (479, 13?)
1.4.4	You've made the work of the Church more difficult (131)

Questions of belief raised by HTG

2.1.1.1	Think again (you're wrong) (2835)

2.1.1.2   You're wrong because of evil influences (54, 9692); You are a false teacher (444)
2.1.2   You must return to Bible truths (498)
2.1.3   Please assure us it is all true (610)
2.2.1   Religion must be true: there are no atheists really; In their hearts humanists want to be in the Church (786)
2.2.2   That I cannot disbelieve (1280)
2.2.3   Reasonable restatement of orthodoxy (1255)
2.2.4   That I cannot believe (2059)
2.2.5   HTG is not radical enough (538)
2.2.6   I question everything (1403)
2.2.7   I seek/sought truth (117, 2641)
2.2.8   As a concerned church member/vicar, I feel I have much in common with intelligent agnostics (135)
2.3   I am an agnostic (714)
2.4.1   Archaic dogma and conceptual imagery today isn't credible (164, 1851, 289)
2.4.2   Dogma just ceased to be credible (2423)
2.5.1   Truth must be scientifically verified (2665)
2.5.2   I am an atheist (2665)
2.6.1   I became a humanist (2423)
2.6.2   I am a humanist (2120)
2.7   HTG is incomprehensible to rationalists (711)
2.8   Man creates God in his own image; Projection theory (378)
2.9   Virulent anti-religion position (947)
2.10   You've taken something away, what have you left us with? (1438, 518)
2.11   I agree, but the consequences will be revolutionary (2366, 621)
2.12   I agree, but where do we go from here? (1403)
2.13   I agree, but reform must come from the laity (2893)
2.14   We must have some image of God (1551)
2.15   Man's image of God fits his time (418)
2.16   It does not matter what you call God – Zeus, Buddha, etc. – all mean the same (perennial philosophy) (857)
2.17   How do we present sophisticated religious beliefs/problems to young people? (2416) (2439) (2444)

The experience of God

3.1.1   Belief in God makes life beautiful/meaningful (2463)
3.1.2   So many good things prove God exists (620, 1595)
3.1.3   Deus ex machina (2071)

3.1.4   God is an abstract principle/mathematics (623)
3.2.1   God is essentially indefinable/ineffable (1254, 366)
3.2.2   God is the more powerful spirit than the spirit that is me (366); Immanentism (457)
3.2.3.1   A spiritual, eternal dimension here and now (950); Transcendentalism
3.2.3.2   The doctrine of the Trinity reconciles/bypasses the problem of the immanent and transcendent God (1002)
3.2.4.1   God is all that is good (11162); Pantheism (1183)
3.2.4.2   I have had the emotional experience of the depth of God's love (1752, 2774)
3.2.4.3   Love is the basic law of the universe (117)
3.2.4.4   The questions of Eros, Philia, and Agape (1198)
3.2.5   We worship God by loving our fellow-men (2286)
3.2.6   The most important thing is to follow the ethical example of Jesus (2368, 3097)
3.2.7   God exists only in the hearts of men (814) (1715); If the world ceased to exist would God still be?
3.3   Atheist or non-church-goer but experiences the need for religious practice (1862)
3.4.1   I have written/am writing under divine inspiration (452)
3.4.2   I have seen a vision (530)
3.4.3   Standard conversion experience (twice born) (490)
3.4.4   God has spoken to me (490)

Sources of ultimate meaning

4.1.1   Authenticity is found only through inner experience (1768)
4.1.2   Mysticism and mystical experience (276)
4.2   Self-realization is the sole source of authenticity (1778)
4.3   Self-denial as the supreme good (1466)
4.4   It's more consistent with man's dignity to live without hopes of eternity (1721)
4.5   People are born with an inherent tendency to worship a supreme being (499)
4.6   Secular man doesn't think about the meaning of life (344)
4.7   Today's God is Money power (686)

Other specific beliefs

5.1.1   Quasi-scientific theories (711)

5.1.2   Christian Science (295)
5.2.1   Reincarnation (366)
5.2.2   Spiritualism (2850, 1678)
5.2.3   Angelology (97)
5.3   The answer to the questions you raise is 'x' (727)
5.4   I am a Jehovah's Witness (1512)
5.5   Quakerism; I'm a Quaker: aren't you really one too? (2953)
5.6   Buddhism; I am a Buddhist (2639)
5.7   Animism (3156); Worship of things/places as God
5.8   Unitarian response (1134)
5.9   Incoherent letters opaque to any systematic analysis (48, 100)
5.10   Manicheism/Zoroastrianism (102)
5.11   Jewish response to HTG (1151, 957)
5.12   Fatalism (235)
5.13   Dialectical materialism (243)
5.14   Christian Socialism (794)
5.15   Rudolph Steiner (737, 644)
5.16   British Israelites (609)
5.17   Philosphical Monism (1044)
5.18   Astrology (1064)
5.19   Catholic (1135)
5.20   Evangelism and its problems of spreading the Gospel (1731)
5.21   Theosophy (1897)

Faith

6.1.1   Faith should be simple; Faith of a little child (42, 516)
6.1.2   Modern trends in theology are anti-Christian when they derogate the unintelligent (3015)
6.2   Ordinary people need a simple faith (even if we don't) (746)
6.3   The simple faith of ordinary people is ignorance and witchcraft (196)
6.4   A simple faith is no longer necessary to maintain social control (213)
6.5   Faith works for psychological reasons (423)
6.6   What is a myth? (1004)
6.7   The doctrine of Materialism is the real evil (1406)

The possibility of religion

7.1.1   If the ground of our being is a psychological category, will science eventually explain it fully? (1891)

7.1.2   If the subconscious mind influences rational behaviour man must commit himself to the will of God or his subconscious will be open to attack from every quarter (3105)

7.2.1   Religion retreats in the face of science (1773)

7.2.2   Religion and Science require different methodologies (1251)

7.3.1   Man is come of age (1051)

7.3.2   Man is not come of age (482)

7.4   If God is immanent how do we transcend death? (868)

7.5   Just to define God does not prove He exists (nominalist v. realist) (1802)

Theodicy

8.1   If God is good why is there suffering? (2222)

8.2   In spite of all the suffering there is also much good (202)

8.3   Evil is brought about by the Devil (399)

8.4   Evil/chaos exists because God isn't omnipotent (2704)

8.5   Evil is unreal (452); Bad things are natural consequences of natural happenings (1506)

8.6   As free will is only apparent we're not responsible for the unintended evil consequences of our acts (102)

8.7   In the face of evil/suffering either you conclude that God's not there or that God's not what you thought (102)

8.8   We shall reap what we sow (264); Karma

8.9   Humble acceptance of suffering (439)

8.10   Man can suffer more than Jesus (853)

8.11   Suffering sharpens religious perception (1293)

Prayer

9.1   How do you pray to 'ultimate reality'/'ground of being'? (1438, 518)

9.2   Prayer is the central issue (545)

9.3   I pray through creative work rather than words (19, 1404)

9.4   Spontaneous prayers or meditation are better than set prayers in church (114, 112)

9.5   The benefits of prayer are subjective in nature (174)

9.6   Prayers are answered (354)

The Church

10.1   Churches should be more like the Samaritans (3139)

10.2   Nominal Christian (3139)

10.3   Christians should be more tolerant of other faiths and other beliefs (1773)

10.4.1   The Church is peripheral, irrelevant; the Church does not speak to modern man (950)

10.4.2   How do we change Church forms without damaging content? (587)

10.5.1   The Church is rotten to the core and needs a new reformation (1960)

10.5.2   We want not a revived church but no Church at all (208)

10.6.1   The Church gets in the way of God (1256)

10.6.2   The Church is the corruptible/fallible form of religion and can be mistaken for the true spiritual substance (3105)

10.7   Church should be separate from State (378)

10.8.1   A priest should work in and among the community he is to lead (2591)

10.8.2   All clergy should be called of God (twice born) (786)

10.9   The Church discriminates against women (1506, 1484, 96, 1072, 1464)

10.10   You have promoted church unity (3153)

10.11   All church leaders and good men should unite to secure world peace, etc. (378)

10.12   The history of the Church is one of wars, massacres and persecutions (111)

Ethics

11.1.1   The Church's ethical teachings are inadequate/out-of-date (680), 2286)

11.1.2   Human relationships (sexual) are adversely affected by the Church's teaching (1576)

11.2.1   Concern with growing permissiveness (726)

11.2.2   We are in danger of throwing out our ethics with the mythological bath water (213)

11.3   Eschatological significance of moral decadence (2082)

11.4   Optimistic view of man's moral evolution (997)

11.5   Evil acts contribute to Christ's perpetual crucifixion (40)
11.6   Individuals/nations should turn the other cheek to aggression (99)
11.7   I am a sinner (355)
11.8   I reject/accept original sin (1044)
11.9   The forms of divine justice (1256)

The Bible

12.1   The Bible is an obscene book (311)
12.2   The Bible is my religion (498)
12.3   The Bible is unsound (1584)

Christology

13.1   Christ was God (551)
13.2   Christ was a prophet not God incarnate (473, 472)
13.3   Christocentrism (666)
13.4   Jesus was the best, but not unique revelation of God (616, 617)
13.5   We are all sons and daughters of God just as Jesus was *the* son of God (872)
13.6   Christ was the Son of God (1331)

Index

Abelard, Peter, 19-20, 21
'Abide with Me', 65
Abraham, 58
'All Through the Night', 65
Anabaptist sects, 34
Anglican Church, *see* Church of
    England
'Aryans', 106
Auschwitz, 63
'Ave Maria', 65

Bainbridge, William Sims, 6, 8, 9
Barrie, J.M., 66
BBC, 87, 88, 92
Beatles, The, 90
Belief, *see* Cognitive style
Bellah, Robert, 4
Berger, Peter, 8, 91
Berkeley, University of California, 8
Bible, the, 97-8; traditionalism and,
    84, 89-90
Bishop of Woolwich, *see* Robinson, Dr
    J.A.T.
'Bless this House', 65
Boys' Brigade, 37
Brave New World, 104
British Legion, 98
Browning, Robert, 65
Buckingham Palace, 92
Buddha, 19
'Burnt Norton', 41

Calvinism, 5, 27
Catholics: Glock and Stark study of,
    13
Certainty and doubt, 100, 101, 104-5;

traditionalism and, 86, 90-1,
    challenge to certainty, 87-8, 91-3
Certitude, 106-7, 108
Chadwick, Owen, 20
Change, 101; traditionalism and, 90-1;
    see also Order and disorder
Choral Evensong, 87
Christ, *see* Jesus
'Christ of St John of the Cross',21
Christian Science, 75
Christology, 19
Church, 97; conversionism and, 44-6,
    48-9; exemplarism and, 24-6, 46;
    gnosticism and, 72, 73, 77-8; theism
    and, 61-2, 66-7; traditionalism and,
    86-7
Church of England, 1, 32, 35, 45, 86
Church of Rome, *see* Roman Catholic
    Church
Civil religion, 4, 108
Cognitive style, 101, 108; conversion-
    ism, of, 46-7; exemplarism, of, 30-1,
    66; faith and, 107; gnosticism, of,
    78; theism, of, 66; traditionalism, of,
    83
Comte, Auguste, 2, 20
Conventional religion, 4, 107, 108, 109
Conversionism: the Church and,
    44-6, 48-9; cognitive style of, 46-7;
    conventional religion, as style of,
    108; conversion, as experience of
    being born again, 43-6, 49-52; evil
    and, 49-50; God and, 41, 47, 50;
    hopelessness of life, and, 40-1; Jesus
    as life-giver, 43-5; prayer and, 48;
    secular culture and, 52-4; sin and,

39-40, 43-4, 51-2; view of past, present and future, and, 41-3
Cupitt, Don, 21

Dali, Salvador, 21
David, 22
Deism, 55
Detroit News, 69
Disorder, *see* Order and disorder
Disraeli, Benjamin, 106
Divine Light Mission, 31
Dornbusch, Stanford, 11
The Dream of Gerontius, 46
Dreyfus Affair, 81
Dualism: gnosticism, in, 70, 72-3, 74, 75
Durkheim, Emile, 2, 3, 17, 27, 34, 51, 81-2, 108

Eckhart, Meister, 21
Eliot, T. S., 41
English Civil War, 34
Epstein, Jacob, 21
Evil: conversionism and, 49-50; gnosticism and, 69, 70-2, 75, 76, 85; theism and, 62-4, 67
Exemplarism: Christian myth, rejection of the, 31-2; the Church, and, 24-6, 46; cognitive style of, 30-1; compared to that of theism, 66; evil and, 28; view of compared to that of conversionism, 49; God, rejection of belief in, 26-8; view of compared to that of theism, 60; heroism, with appeal to the working classes, as, 22-3, 37; hope for the future, in, 30, 68; humanism, as, 28-9; Jesus, the Church, contrasted with, 24; hero figure, as, 19-23, 26, 28-32, 33, 34, 35, 36; comparison with view of conversionism, 38-9, 40-1; life after death, rejection of belief in, 26, 32-4; prayer, lack of belief in, 35; reasons for survival of, 36-7; secular culture and, 34; view of past, present and future compared to that of conversionism, 41-2

The Fairie Queene, 101
Faith, 105-6, 107-8
The Fall of Public Man, 21
'Fantasia on a Theme of Thomas Tallis', 66
Feuerbach, L.A., 56
Fields, Gracie, 65

Forster, E.M., 78
Foss, Hubert, 66
Freud, Sigmund, 2, 33, 56

Geertz, Clifford, 7
Gifford Lectures (1901-2), 10
Glock, Charles, 8, 11, 12, 13, 14
Gnosticism: the Church, and, 72, 73, 77-8; cognitive style of, 78; conventional religion, as style of, 108; dualism in, 70, 72-3, 74, 75; evil and, 69, 70-2, 75, 76, 85; God, idea of, in, 70-2, 73, 74; Jesus and, 74-5; life after death and, 68, 75-6; mysticism and, 69, 73-4; natural world, the, and, 69, 72, 79; prayer and, 72; sin and, 71-2; spiritual world, the, and, 68-9; spiritualism and, 75, 77
God: belief in, 12-13, 94-6; conversionism and, 41, 47; exemplarism's rejection of belief in, 26-8; gnosticism's idea of, 70-2, 73, 74; Jesus and, 59-60, 74, 98; Sky-Father/Earth-Mother figure, as, 55, 56-8, 62
Golding, William, 39
Greeley, Andrew, 6, 8, 11

Hammarskjöld, Dag, 26
Hinduism, 27
Hoggart, Richard, 22-3, 37, 65
Holman Hunt, William, 21
'The Holy City', 65
Honest to God, 15, 88, 91; analysis of letters in response to, 15-18, 94, 98
Hope for the future, 30, 68
Hopelessness of life, 40-1
House of Lords, 86
Humanism: exemplarism as, 28-9
Hunt, William Holman, *see* Holman Hunt, William
Huxley, Aldous

Invisible religion, 4, 108
The Invisible Religion, 2, 3, 5
Islam, 27

James, William, 10-11, 15, 17, 18, 44
Jeremiah, 90
Jesus: the Church, in contrast to, 24; conversionism and, 43-5; development of image of, 19-21; gnosticism and, 74-5; hero figure, as, 19-23, 26, 28-32, 33, 34, 35, 36;

contrasted to view of conversionism, 38-9, 40-1; theism and, 59-60, 61, 66, 67; traditionalism and, 87-8
Job, 64
Judaeo-Christian tradition, 14, 57
Judaism, 27

Keeler, Christine, 90

Lady Chatterley's Lover, 91, 92
Lenski, Gerhard, 13-14, 99
Lewis, C.S., 55
Life after death, 95; exemplarism's rejection of, 26, 32-4; gnosticism and, 68, 75-6
The Life of Christ, 20
The Life of Jesus, 20
'The Light of the World', 21
Llandaff Cathedral, 21
Lord of the Flies, 39
The Lord of the Rings, 32
'The Lord's Prayer', 65
'The Lost Chord', 65
Luckmann, Thomas, 2, 3, 4, 5, 6, 8, 82

McCready, William, 6, 8, 11
Marx, Karl, 2
Maurice, 78
Meaning systems, 5-7, 8-11, 14, 109
Meeting Point, 88
Methodist traditionalism, 86
Mohammed, 19
Morris, Father S. J., 100
Moses, 22, 58
Mothers' Union, 98
Mr Grace, 78
Muller, F. M., 56
Mysticism: gnosticism and, 69, 73-4

Napoleon, 22
Nazi Germany, 106
Needham, Rodney, 30-1
New religious movements, 4, 108
New Testament, 65
Newman, Cardinal John, 46, 101
Noah, 90

'Oh, for the Wings of a Dove', 65
'The Old Rugged Cross', 65
Old Testament, 55, 65
Order and disorder, 101-4
Orthodox Christianity, 98-9

The Phenomenon of Man, 33
Piazza, Thomas, 8, 11

Pius X, Pope, 21
Plymouth Brethren, 31
Pontius Pilate, 38
Popular religion, 4, 108
Popular Religion, 11
Prayer, 97; conversionism and, 48; exemplarism's lack of belief in, 35; gnosticism and, 72; theism and, 66
Promethean myth, 28, 33
Protestants: Glock and Stark study of, 13
Protestants' view of Jesus, 28
Puritan sects, 34

Religion and Society in Tension, 12
Religious experience, studies of, 10-14
The Religious Factor, 13
Renan, Ernest, 20, 21, 25
Ricoeur, Paul, 7
Robinson, Dr J.A.T. (Bishop of Woolwich), 14-15, 17, 55, 72, 74, 84, 94, 99, 107
Roman Catholic Traditionalism, 86
Rousseau, Jean-Jacques, 4
Russell, Bertrand, 100
Russell, Lady Katharine, 100

St Paul, 60, 72, 88
St Peter, 89
Saint-Simon, Claude, 2
St Teresa, 10
Samaritans, The, 37
San Francisco Bay Area survey (1973), 5
Schneider, Louis, 11
Scout Association, 37
Second World War, 32
Sectarian religion, 4, 108
Sennett, Richard, 21
Shakespeare, William, 33
Siegfried, 22
Sims Bainbridge, William, *see* Bainbridge, William Sims
Sin: conversionism and, 39-40, 43-4, 51-2; gnosticism and, 71-2
Sociology of religion, studies on the, 2-14
Sodom, 92
South Africa, Republic of, 106
Spencer, Herbert, 2
Spenser, Edmund, 101
Spiritual world: gnosticism's view of, 68-9, 72, 79
Spiritualism: gnosticism and, 75, 77
Starbuck, E.M., 20

INDEX

Styles of religion, 108-9
Surrogate religion, 4, 108
The Symbolism of Evil, 7

Teilhard de Chardin, Pierre, 33
Temple, William, 39
That Was The Week That Was, 92
Theism: Church and, 61-2, 66-7;
  cognitive style of, 66; death and, 66;
  evil and, 62-4, 67; God and, 55-67;
  Sky-Father/Earth-Mother figure, as,
  55, 56-8, 62; Jesus and, 59-60, 61,
  66, 67; popular culture and, 65;
  prayer and, 66; Western style
  religion, as, 56, 66; the world, and,
  56, 58-9, 62
Thomas, W.L., 11
Tolkein, J.R.R., 32
Tolstoy, Leo, 10
Traditionalism: belief and, 82; the
  Bible, and, 89-90; certainty and, 86,
  90-1; challenge to, and, 87-8, 91-3;
  change and, 90-1; characteristics of,
  81; the Church, and, 86-7; cognitive
  style of, 83-4; conservation, idea of,
  and, 82-3; Jesus and, 87, 88;
  resurrection, importance of, and,
  88-9, 90; morality and, 92-3; society
  and, 85-6
Traherne, Thomas, 58
Trilling, Lionel, 21
Tristan, 22
Turner, Victor, 57

The Uses of Literacy, 22-3

The Varieties of Religious Experience,
  10, 18
Vaughan Williams, Ralph, 66
Vidler, Alec, 92

Wagner, Richard, 32
Weber, Max, 2, 5, 17, 19, 48, 57, 70,
  99
Wellington, 22
Williams, Ralph Vaughan, *see*
  Vaughan Williams, Ralph
Wordsworth, William, 58, 65
Wuthnow, Robert, 5, 6, 7, 8, 9, 10, 11

Znaniecki, F., 11
Zoroaster, 19

Routledge Social Science Series

Routledge & Kegan Paul
London, Boston, Melbourne and Henley

39 Store Street, London WC1E 7DD
9 Park Street, Boston, Mass 02108
296 Beaconsfield Parade, Middle Park,
Melbourne, 3206 Australia
Broadway House, Newtown Road,
Henley-on-Thames, Oxon RG9 1EN

Contents

International Library of Sociology 2
General Sociology 2
Foreign Classics of Sociology 3
Social Structure 3
Sociology and Politics 4
Criminology 4
Social Psychology 5
Sociology of the Family 5
Social Services 5
Sociology of Education 6
Sociology of Culture 6
Sociology of Religion 7
Sociology of Art and Literature 7
Sociology of Knowledge 7
Urban Sociology 7
Rural Sociology 8
*Sociology of Industry and
Distribution* 8
Anthropology 8
Sociology and Philosophy 9

International Library of
Anthropology 9
International Library of Phenomen-
ology and Moral Sciences 10
International Library of Social
Policy 10
International Library of Welfare and
Philosophy 11
Library of Social Work 11
Primary Socialization, Language and
Education 13
Reports of the Institute of
Community Studies 13
Reports of the Institute for Social
Studies in Medical Care 14
Medicine, Illness and Society 14
Monographs in Social Theory 14
Routledge Social Science Journals 14
Social and Psychological Aspects of
Medical Practice 15

*Authors wishing to submit manuscripts for any series
in this catalogue should send them to the Social Science Editor,
Routledge & Kegan Paul plc, 39 Store Street,
London WC1E 7DD.*
● *Books so marked are available in paperback also.*
○ *Books so marked are available in paperback only.*
*All books are in metric Demy 8vo format (216 × 138mm approx.)
unless otherwise stated.*

International Library of Sociology
General Editor John Rex

GENERAL SOCIOLOGY

Alexander, J. Theoretical Logic in Sociology.
  Volume 1: Positivism, Presuppositions and Current Controversies. *234 pp.*
  Volume 2: The Antinomies of Classical Thought: *Marx and Durkheim.*
  Volume 3: The Classical Attempt at Theoretical Synthesis: *Max Weber.*
  Volume 4: The Modern Reconstruction of Classical Thought: *Talcott Parsons.*
Barnsley, J. H. The Social Reality of Ethics. *464 pp.*
Brown, Robert. Explanation in Social Science. *208 pp.*
● Rules and Laws in Sociology. *192 pp.*
Bruford, W. H. Chekhov and His Russia. *A Sociological Study. 244 pp.*
Burton, F. and **Carlen, P.** Official Discourse. *On Discourse Analysis, Government Publications, Ideology. 160 pp.*
Cain, Maureen E. Society and the Policeman's Role. *326 pp.*
● **Fletcher, Colin.** Beneath the Surface. *An Account of Three Styles of Sociological Research. 221 pp.*
Gibson, Quentin. The Logic of Social Enquiry. *240 pp.*
Glassner, B. Essential Interactionism. *208 pp.*
Glucksmann, M. Structuralist Analysis in Contemporary Social Thought. *212 pp.*
Gurvitch, Georges. Sociology of Law. *Foreword by Roscoe Pound. 264 pp.*
Hinkle, R. Founding Theory of American Sociology 1881–1913. *376 pp.*
Homans, George C. Sentiments and Activities. *336 pp.*
Johnson, Harry M. Sociology: *A Systematic Introduction. Foreword by Robert K. Merton. 710 pp.*
● **Keat, Russell** and **Urry, John.** Social Theory as Science. *Second Edition. 278 pp.*
Mannheim, Karl. Essays on Sociology and Social Psychology. *Edited by Paul Keckskemeti. With Editorial Note by Adolph Lowe. 344 pp.*
Martindale, Don. The Nature and Types of Sociological Theory. *292 pp.*
● **Maus, Heinz.** A Short History of Sociology. *234 pp.*
Merquior, J. G. Rousseau and Weber. *A Study in the Theory of Legitimacy. 240 pp.*
Myrdal, Gunnar. Value in Social Theory: *A Collection of Essays on Methodology. Edited by Paul Streeten. 332 pp.*
Ogburn, William F. and **Nimkoff, Meyer F.** A Handbook of Sociology. *Preface by Karl Mannheim. 656 pp. 46 figures. 35 tables.*
Parsons, Talcott and **Smelser, Neil J.** Economy and Society: *A Study in the Integration of Economic and Social Theory. 362 pp.*
Payne, G., Dingwall, R., Payne, J. and **Carter, M.** Sociology and Social Research. *336 pp.*
Podgórecki, A. Practical Social Sciences. *144 pp.*
Podgórecki, A. and **Łos, M.** Multidimensional Sociology. *268 pp.*
Raffel, S. Matters of Fact. *A Sociological Inquiry. 152 pp.*
● **Rex, John.** Key Problems of Sociological Theory. *220 pp.*
  Sociology and the Demystification of the Modern World. *282 pp.*
● **Rex, John.** (Ed.) Approaches to Sociology. *Contributions by Peter Abell, Frank Bechhofer, Basil Bernstein, Ronald Fletcher, David Frisby, Miriam Glucksmann, Peter Lassman, Herminio Martins, John Rex, Roland Robertson, John Westergaard and Jock Young. 302 pp.*
Rigby, A. Alternative Realities. *352 pp.*
Roche, M. Phenomenology, Language and the Social Sciences. *374 pp.*
Sahay, A. Sociological Analysis. *220 pp.*
Strasser, Hermann. The Normative Structure of Sociology. *Conservative and Emancipatory Themes in Social Thought. 286 pp.*

Strong, P. Ceremonial Order of the Clinic. *267 pp.*
Urry, J. Reference Groups and the Theory of Revolution. *244 pp.*
Weinberg, E. Development of Sociology in the Soviet Union. *173 pp.*

FOREIGN CLASSICS OF SOCIOLOGY

● Gerth, H. H. and Mills, C. Wright. From Max Weber: *Essays in Sociology.*
  502 pp.
● Tönnies, Ferdinand. Community and Association (*Gemeinschaft und Gesell-schaft*). *Translated and Supplemented by Charles P. Loomis. Foreword by
  Pitirim A. Sorokin. 334 pp.*

SOCIAL STRUCTURE

Andreski, Stanislav. Military Organization and Society. *Foreword by Professor
  A. R. Radcliffe-Brown. 226 pp. 1 folder.*
Bozzoli, B. The Political Nature of a Ruling Class. *Capital and Ideology in
  South Africa 1890–1939. 396 pp.*
Bauman, Z. Memories of Class. *The Prehistory and After life of Class. 240 pp.*
Broom, L., Lancaster Jones, F., McDonnell, P. and Williams, T. The
  Inheritance of Inequality. *208 pp.*
Carlton, Eric. Ideology and Social Order. *Foreword by Professor Philip
  Abrahams. 326 pp.*
Clegg, S. and Dunkerley, D. Organization, Class and Control. *614 pp.*
Coontz, Sydney H. Population Theories and the Economic Interpretation. *202 pp.*
Coser, Lewis. The Functions of Social Conflict. *204 pp.*
Crook, I. and D. The First Years of the Yangyi Commune. *304 pp., illustrated.*
Dickie-Clark, H. F. Marginal Situation: *A Sociological Study of a Coloured
  Group. 240 pp. 11 tables.*
Fidler, J. The British Business Elite. *Its Attitudes to Class, Status and Power.
  332 pp.*
Giner, S. and Archer, M. S. (Eds) Contemporary Europe: *Social Structures and
  Cultural Patterns. 336 pp.*
● Glaser, Barney and Strauss, Anselm L. Status Passage: *A Formal Theory.
  212 pp.*
Glass, D. V. (Ed.) Social Mobility in Britain. *Contributions by J. Berent,
  T. Bottomore, R. C. Chambers, J. Floud, D. V. Glass, J. R. Hall, H. T.
  Himmelweit, R. K. Kelsall, F. M. Martin, C. A. Moser, R. Mukherjee and
  W. Ziegel. 420 pp.*
Kelsall, R. K. Higher Civil Servants in Britain: *From 1870 to the Present Day.
  268 pp. 31 tables.*
● Lawton, Denis. Social Class, Language and Education. *192 pp.*
McLeish, John. The Theory of Social Change. *Four Views Considered. 128 pp.*
● Marsh, David C. The Changing Social Structure of England and Wales,
  1871–1961. *Revised edition. 288 pp.*
Menzies, Ken. Talcott Parsons and the Social Image of Man. *206 pp.*
● Mouzelis, Nicos. Organization and Bureaucracy. *An Analysis of Modern
  Theories. 240 pp.*
● Ossowski, Stanislaw. Class Structure in the Social Consciousness. *210 pp.*
● Podgórecki, Adam. Law and Society. *302 pp.*
Ratcliffe, P. Racism and Reaction. *A Profile of Handsworth. 388 pp.*
Renner, Karl. Institutions of Private Law and Their Social Functions. *Edited,
  with an Introduction and Notes, by O. Kahn-Freud. Translated by Agnes
  Schwarzschild. 316 pp.*
Rex, J. and Tomlinson, S. Colonial Immigrants in a British City. *A Class
  Analysis. 368 pp.*
Smooha, S. Israel. *Pluralism and Conflict. 472 pp.*
Strasser, H. and Randall, S. C. An Introduction to Theories of Social Change.
  300 pp.

Wesolowski, W. Class, Strata and Power. *Trans. and with Introduction by G. Kolankiewicz. 160 pp.*

Zureik, E. Palestinians in Israel. *A Study in Internal Colonialism. 264 pp.*

SOCIOLOGY AND POLITICS

Acton, T. A. Gypsy Politics and Social Change. *316 pp.*

Burton, F. Politics of Legitimacy. *Struggles in a Belfast Community. 250 pp.*

Crook, I. and D. Revolution in a Chinese Village. *Ten Mile Inn. 216 pp., illustrated.*

de Silva, S. B. D. The Political Economy of Underdevelopment. *640 pp.*

Etzioni-Halevy, E. Political Manipulation and Administrative Power. *A Comparative Study. 228 pp.*

Fielding, N. The National Front. *260 pp.*

● Hechter, Michael. Internal Colonialism. *The Celtic Fringe in British National Development, 1536–1966. 380 pp.*

Levy, N. The Foundations of the South African Cheap Labour System. *367 pp.*

Kornhauser, William. The Politics of Mass Society. *272 pp. 20 tables.*

● Korpi, W. The Working Class in Welfare Capitalism. *Work, Unions and Politics in Sweden. 472 pp.*

Kroes, R. Soldiers and Students. *A Study of Right- and Left-wing Students. 174 pp.*

Martin, Roderick. Sociology of Power. *214 pp.*

Merquior, J. G. Rousseau and Weber. *A Study in the Theory of Legitimacy. 286 pp.*

Myrdal, Gunnar. The Political Element in the Development of Economic Theory. *Translated from the German by Paul Streeten. 282 pp.*

Preston, P. W. Theories of Development. *296 pp.*

Varma, B. N. The Sociology and Politics of Development. *A Theoretical Study. 236 pp.*

Wong, S.-L. Sociology and Socialism in Contemporary China. *160 pp.*

Wootton, Graham. Workers, Unions and the State. *188 pp.*

CRIMINOLOGY

Ancel, Marc. Social Defence: *A Modern Approach to Criminal Problems. Foreword by Leon Radzinowicz. 240 pp.*

Athens, L. Violent Criminal Acts and Actors. *104 pp.*

Cain, Maureen E. Society and the Policeman's Role. *326 pp.*

Cloward, Richard A. and Ohlin, Lloyd E. Delinquency and Opportunity: *A Theory of Delinquent Gangs. 248 pp.*

Downes, David M. The Delinquent Solution. *A Study in Subcultural Theory. 296 pp.*

Friedlander, Kate. The Psycho-Analytical Approach to Juvenile Delinquency: *Theory, Case Studies, Treatment. 320 pp.*

Gleuck, Sheldon and Eleanor. Family Environment and Delinquency. *With the statistical assistance of Rose W. Kneznek. 340 pp.*

Lopez-Rey, Manuel. Crime. *An Analytical Appraisal. 288 pp.*

Mannheim, Hermann. Comparative Criminology: *A Text Book. Two volumes. 442 pp. and 380 pp.*

Morris, Terence. The Criminal Area: *A Study in Social Ecology. Foreword by Hermann Mannheim. 232 pp. 25 tables. 4 maps.*

Rock, Paul. Making People Pay. *338 pp.*

● Taylor, Ian, Walton, Paul and Young, Jock. The New Criminology. *For a Social Theory of Deviance. 325 pp.*

● Taylor, Ian, Walton, Paul and Young, Jock. (Eds) Critical Criminology. *268 pp.*

SOCIAL PSYCHOLOGY

Bagley, Christopher. The Social Psychology of the Epileptic Child. *320 pp.*
Brittan, Arthur. Meanings and Situations. *224 pp.*
Carroll, J. Break-Out from the Crystal Palace. *200 pp.*
● **Fleming, C. M.** Adolescence: Its Social Psychology. *With an Introduction to recent findings from the fields of Anthropology, Physiology, Medicine, Psychometrics and Sociometry. 288 pp.*
● The Social Psychology of Education: *An Introduction and Guide to Its Study. 136 pp.*
Linton, Ralph. The Cultural Background of Personality. *132 pp.*
● **Mayo, Elton.** The Social Problems of an Industrial Civilization. *With an Appendix on the Political Problem. 180 pp.*
Ottaway, A. K. C. Learning Through Group Experience. *176 pp.*
Plummer, Ken. Sexual Stigma. *An Interactionist Account. 254 pp.*
● **Rose, Arnold M.** (Ed.) Human Behaviour and Social Processes: *an Interactionist Approach. Contributions by Arnold M. Rose, Ralph H. Turner, Anselm Strauss, Everett C. Hughes, E. Franklin Frazier, Howard S. Becker et al. 696 pp.*
Smelser, Neil J. Theory of Collective Behaviour. *448 pp.*
Stephenson, Geoffrey M. The Development of Conscience. *128 pp.*
Young, Kimball. Handbook of Social Psychology. *658 pp. 16 figures. 10 tables.*

SOCIOLOGY OF THE FAMILY

Bell, Colin R. Middle Class Families: *Social and Geographical Mobility. 224 pp.*
Burton, Lindy. Vulnerable Children. *272 pp.*
Gavron, Hannah. The Captive Wife: *Conflicts of Household Mothers. 190 pp.*
George, Victor and **Wilding, Paul.** Motherless Families. *248 pp.*
Klein, Josephine. Samples from English Cultures.
    1. Three Preliminary Studies and Aspects of Adult Life in England. *447 pp.*
    2. Child-Rearing Practices and Index. *247 pp.*
Klein, Viola. The Feminine Character. *History of an Ideology. 244 pp.*
McWhinnie, Alexina M. Adopted Children. *How They Grow Up. 304 pp.*
● **Morgan, D. H. J.** Social Theory and the Family. *188 pp.*
● **Myrdal, Alva** and **Klein, Viola.** Women's Two Roles: *Home and Work. 238 pp. 27 tables.*
Parsons, Talcott and **Bales, Robert F.** Family: Socialization and Interaction Process. *In collaboration with James Olds, Morris Zelditch and Philip E. Slater. 456 pp. 50 figures and tables.*

SOCIAL SERVICES

Bastide, Roger. The Sociology of Mental Disorder. *Translated from the French by Jean McNeil. 260 pp.*
Carlebach, Julius. Caring for Children in Trouble. *266 pp.*
George, Victor. Foster Care. *Theory and Practice. 234 pp.*
    Social Security: *Beveridge and After. 258 pp.*
George, V. and **Wilding, P.** Motherless Families. *248 pp.*
● **Goetschius, George W.** Working with Community Groups. *256 pp.*
Goetschius, George W. and **Tash, Joan.** Working with Unattached Youth. *416 pp.*
Heywood, Jean S. Children in Care. *The Development of the Service for the Deprived Child. Third revised edition. 284 pp.*
King, Roy D., Ranes, Norma V. and **Tizard, Jack.** Patterns of Residential Care. *356 pp.*
Leigh, John. Young People and Leisure. *256 pp.*
● **Mays, John.** (Ed.) Penelope Hall's Social Services of England and Wales. *368 pp.*

Morris Mary. Voluntary Work and the Welfare State. *300 pp.*
Nokes. P. L. The Professional Task in Welfare Practice. *152 pp.*
Timms, Noel. Psychiatric Social Work in Great Britain (1939–1962). *280 pp.*
● Social Casework: *Principles and Practice. 256 pp.*

SOCIOLOGY OF EDUCATION

Banks, Olive. Parity and Prestige in English Secondary Education: a Study in Educational Sociology. *272 pp.*
● **Blyth, W. A. L.** English Primary Education. *A Sociological Description.* 2. Background. *168 pp.*
Collier, K. G. The Social Purposes of Education: *Personal and Social Values in Education. 268 pp.*
Evans, K. M. Sociometry and Education. *158 pp.*
● **Ford, Julienne.** Social Class and the Comprehensive School. *192 pp.*
Foster, P. J. Education and Social Change in Ghana. *336 pp. 3 maps.*
Fraser, W. R. Education and Society in Modern France. *150 pp.*
Grace, Gerald R. Role Conflict and the Teacher. *150 pp.*
Hans, Nicholas. New Trends in Education in the Eighteenth Century. *278 pp. 19 tables.*
● Comparative Education: *A Study of Educational Factors and Traditions. 360 pp.*
● **Hargreaves, David.** Interpersonal Relations and Education. *432 pp.*
● Social Relations in a Secondary School. *240 pp.*
School Organization and Pupil Involvement. *A Study of Secondary Schools.*
● **Mannheim, Karl** and **Stewart, W. A. C.** An Introduction to the Sociology of Education. *206 pp.*
● **Musgrove, F.** Youth and the Social Order. *176 pp.*
● **Ottaway, A. K. C.** Education and Society: An Introduction to the Sociology of Education. *With an Introduction by W. O. Lester Smith. 212 pp.*
Peers, Robert. Adult Education: *A Comparative Study. Revised edition. 398 pp.*
Stratta, Erica. The Education of Borstal Boys. *A Study of their Educational Experiences prior to, and during, Borstal Training. 256 pp.*
● **Taylor, P. H., Reid, W. A.** and **Holley, B. J.** The English Sixth Form. *A Case Study in Curriculum Research. 198 pp.*

SOCIOLOGY OF CULTURE

● **Eppel, E. M.** and **M.** Adolescents and Morality: *A Study of some Moral Values and Dilemmas of Working Adolescents in the Context of a changing Climate of Opinion. Foreword by W. J. H. Sprott. 268 pp. 39 tables.*
● **Fromm, Erich.** The Fear of Freedom. *286 pp.*
● The Sane Society. *400 pp.*
Johnson, L. The Cultural Critics. *From Matthew Arnold to Raymond Williams. 233 pp.*
Mannheim, Karl. Essays on the Sociology of Culture. *Edited by Ernst Mannheim in co-operation with Paul Kecskemeti. Editorial Note by Adolph Lowe. 280 pp.*
Structures of Thinking. *Edited by David Kettler, Volker Meja and Nico Stehr. 304 pp.*
Merquior, J. G. The Veil and the Mask. *Essays on Culture and Ideology. Foreword by Ernest Gellner. 140 pp.*
Zijderfeld, A. C. On Clichés. *The Supersedure of Meaning by Function in Modernity. 150 pp.*
Reality in a Looking Glass. *Rationality through an Analysis of Traditional Folly. 208 pp.*

SOCIOLOGY OF RELIGION

Argyle, Michael and **Beit-Hallahmi, Benjamin.** The Social Psychology of
    Religion. *256 pp.*
Glasner, Peter E. The Sociology of Secularisation. *A Critique of a Concept.*
    146 pp.
Hall, J. R. The Ways Out. *Utopian Communal Groups in an Age of Babylon.*
    280 pp.
Ranson, S., Hinings, B. and **Bryman, A.** Clergy, Ministers and Priests. *216 pp.*
Stark, Werner. The Sociology of Religion. *A Study of Christendom.*
    Volume II. *Sectarian Religion. 368 pp.*
    Volume III. *The Universal Church. 464 pp.*
    Volume IV. *Types of Religious Man. 352 pp.*
    Volume V. *Types of Religious Culture. 464 pp.*
Turner, B. S. Weber and Islam. *216 pp.*
Watt, W. Montgomery. Islam and the Integration of Society. 230 pp.
Pomian-Srzednicki, M. Religious Change in Contemporary Poland. *Sociology*
    and Secularization. 280 pp.

SOCIOLOGY OF ART AND LITERATURE

Jarvie, Ian C. Towards a Sociology of the Cinema. *A Comparative Essay on the*
    Structure and Functioning of a Major Entertainment Industry. 405 pp.
Rust, Frances S. Dance in Society. *An Analysis of the Relationships between the*
    Social Dance and Society in England from the Middle Ages to the Present
    Day. 256 pp. 8 pp. of plates.
Schücking, L. L. The Sociology of Literary Taste. *112 pp.*
Wolff, Janet. Hermeneutic Philosophy and the Sociology of Art. *150 pp.*

SOCIOLOGY OF KNOWLEDGE

Diesing, P. Patterns of Discovery in the Social Sciences. *262 pp.*
● **Douglas, J. D.** (Ed.) Understanding Everyday Life. *270 pp.*
● **Hamilton, P.** Knowledge and Social Structure. *174 pp.*
Jarvie, I. C. Concepts and Society. *232 pp.*
Mannheim, Karl. Essays on the Sociology of Knowledge. *Edited by Paul*
    Kecskemeti. Editorial Note by Adolph Lowe. 353 pp.
Remmling, Gunter W. The Sociology of Karl Mannheim. *With a*
    Bibliographical Guide to the Sociology of Knowledge, Ideological Analysis,
    and Social Planning. 255 pp.
Remmling, Gunter W. (Ed.) Towards the Sociology of Knowledge. *Origin and*
    Development of a Sociological Thought Style. 463 pp.
Scheler, M. Problems of a Sociology of Knowledge. *Trans. by M. S. Frings.*
    Edited and with an Introduction by K. Stikkers. 232 pp.

URBAN SOCIOLOGY

Aldridge, M. The British New Towns. *A Programme Without a Policy. 232 pp.*
Ashworth, William. The Genesis of Modern British Town Planning: *A Study in*
    Economic and Social History of the Nineteenth and Twentieth Centuries.
    288 pp.
Brittan, A. The Privatised World. *196 pp.*
Cullingworth, J. B. Housing Needs and Planning Policy: *a Restatement of the*
    Problems of Housing Need and 'Overspill' in England and Wales. 232 pp.
    44 tables. 8 maps.
Dickinson, Robert E. City and Region: *A Geographical Interpretation. 608 pp.*
    125 figures.
    The West European City: *A Geographical Interpretation. 600 pp. 129 maps.*
    29 plates.

8

Humphreys, Alexander J. New Dubliners: *Urbanization and the Irish Family.* *Foreword by George C. Homans. 304 pp.*

Jackson, Brian. Working Class Community: *Some General Notions raised by a Series of Studies in Northern England. 192 pp.*

● **Mann, P. H.** An Approach to Urban Sociology. *240 pp.*

Mellor, J. R. Urban Sociology in an Urbanized Society. *326 pp.*

Morris, R. N. and **Mogey, J.** The Sociology of Housing. *Studies at Berinsfield. 232 pp. 4 pp. plates.*

Mullan, R. Stevenage Ltd. *438 pp.*

Rex, J. and **Tomlinson, S.** Colonial Immigrants in a British City. *A Class Analysis. 368 pp.*

Rosser, C. and **Harris, C.** The Family and Social Change. *A Study of Family and Kinship in a South Wales Town. 352 pp. 8 maps.*

● **Stacey, Margaret, Batsone, Eric, Bell, Colin** and **Thurcott, Anne.** Power, Persistence and Change. *A Second Study of Banbury. 196 pp.*

RURAL SOCIOLOGY

● **Mayer, Adrian C.** Peasants in the Pacific. *A Study of Fiji Indian Rural Society. 248 pp. 20 plates.*

Williams, W. M. The Sociology of an English Village: *Gosforth. 272 pp. 12 figures. 13 tables.*

SOCIOLOGY OF INDUSTRY AND DISTRIBUTION

Dunkerley, David. The Foreman. *Aspects of Task and Structure. 192 pp.*

Eldridge, J. E. T. Industrial Disputes. *Essays in the Sociology of Industrial Relations. 288 pp.*

Hollowell, Peter G. The Lorry Driver. *272 pp.*

● **Oxaal, I., Barnett, T.** and **Booth, D.** (Eds) Beyond the Sociology of Development. *Economy and Society in Latin America and Africa. 295 pp.*

Smelser, Neil J. Social Change in the Industrial Revolution: *An Application of Theory to the Lancashire Cotton Industry, 1770–1840. 468 pp. 12 figures. 14 tables.*

Watson, T. J. The Personnel Managers. *A Study in the Sociology of Work and Employment, 262 pp.*

ANTHROPOLOGY

Brandel-Syrier, Mia. Reeftown Elite. *A Study of Social Mobility in a Modern African Community on the Reef. 376 pp.*

Dickie-Clark, H. F. The Marginal Situation. *A Sociological Study of a Coloured Group. 236 pp.*

Dube, S. C. Indian Village. *Foreword by Morris Edward Opler. 276 pp. 4 plates.*

India's Changing Villages: *Human Factors in Community Development. 260 pp. 8 plates. 1 map.*

Fei, H.-T. Peasant Life in China. *A Field Study of Country Life in the Yangtze Valley. With a foreword by Bronislaw Malinowski. 328 pp. 16 pp. plates.*

Firth, Raymond. Malay Fishermen. *Their Peasant Economy. 420 pp. 17 pp. plates.*

Gulliver, P. H. Social Control in an African Society: a Study of the Arusha, Agricultural Masai of Northern Tanganyika. *320 pp. 8 plates. 10 figures.* Family Herds. *288 pp.*

Jarvie, Ian C. The Revolution in Anthropology. *268 pp.*

Little, Kenneth L. Mende of Sierra Leone. *308 pp. and folder.*

Negroes in Britain. *With a New Introduction and Contemporary Study by Leonard Bloom. 320 pp.*

Tambs-Lyche, H. London Patidars. *168 pp.*
Madan, G. R. Western Sociologists on Indian Society. *Marx, Spencer, Weber, Durkheim, Pareto. 384 pp.*
Mayer, A. C. Peasants in the Pacific. *A Study of Fiji Indian Rural Society. 248 pp.*
Meer, Fatima. Race and Suicide in South Africa. *325 pp.*
Smith, Raymond T. The Negro Family in British Guiana: *Family Structure and Social Status in the Villages. With a Foreword by Meyer Fortes. 314 pp. 8 plates. 1 figure. 4 maps.*

SOCIOLOGY AND PHILOSOPHY

● **Adriaansens, H.** Talcott Parsons and the Conceptual Dilemma. *200 pp.*
Barnsley, John H. The Social Reality of Ethics. *A Comparative Analysis of Moral Codes. 448 pp.*
Diesing, Paul. Patterns of Discovery in the Social Sciences. *362 pp.*
● **Douglas, Jack D.** (Ed.) Understanding Everyday Life. *Toward the Reconstruction of Sociological Knowledge. Contributions by Alan F. Blum, Aaron W. Cicourel, Norman K. Denzin, Jack D. Douglas, John Heeren, Peter McHugh, Peter K. Manning, Melvin Power, Matthew Speier, Roy Turner, D. Lawrence Wieder, Thomas P. Wilson and Don H. Zimmerman. 370 pp.*
Gorman, Robert A. The Dual Vision. *Alfred Schutz and the Myth of Phenomenological Social Science. 240 pp.*
Jarvie, Ian C. Concepts and Society. *216 pp.*
Kilminster, R. Praxis and Method. *A Sociological Dialogue with Lukács, Gramsci and the Early Frankfurt School. 334 pp.*
Outhwaite, W. Concept Formation in Social Science. *255 pp.*
● **Pelz, Werner.** The Scope of Understanding in Sociology. *Towards a More Radical Reorientation in the Social Humanistic Sciences. 283 pp.*
Roche, Maurice, Phenomenology, Language and the Social Sciences. *371 pp.*
Sahay, Arun. Sociological Analysis. *212 pp.*
● **Slater, P.** Origin and Significance of the Frankfurt School. *A Marxist Perspective. 185 pp.*
Spurling, L. Phenomenology and the Social World. *The Philosophy of Merleau-Ponty and its Relation to the Social Sciences. 222 pp.*
Wilson, H. T. The American Ideology. *Science, Technology and Organization as Modes of Rationality. 368 pp.*

International Library of Anthropology
General Editor Adam Kuper

● **Ahmed, A. S.** Millennium and Charisma Among Pathans. *A Critical Essay in Social Anthropology. 192 pp.*
Pukhtun Economy and Society. *Traditional Structure and Economic Development. 422 pp.*
Barth, F. Selected Essays. *Volume 1. 256 pp.* Selected Essays. *Volume II. 200 pp.*
Brown, Paula. The Chimbu. *A Study of Change in the New Guinea Highlands. 151 pp.*
Duller, H. J. Development Technology. *192 pp.*
Foner, N. Jamaica Farewell. *200 pp.*
Gudeman, Stephen. Relationships, Residence and the Individual. *A Rural Panamanian Community. 288 pp. 11 plates, 5 figures, 2 maps, 10 tables.*
The Demise of a Rural Economy. *From Subsistence to Capitalism in a Latin American Village. 160 pp.*

Hamnett, Ian. Chieftainship and Legitimacy. *An Anthropological Study of Executive Law in Lesotho. 163 pp.*
Hanson, F. Allan. Meaning in Culture. *127 pp.*
Hazan, H. The Limbo People. *A Study of the Constitution of the Time Universe Among the Aged. 208 pp.*
Humphreys, S. C. Anthropology and the Greeks. *288 pp.*
Karp, I. Fields of Change Among the Iteso of Kenya. *140 pp.*
Kuper, A. Wives for Cattle. *Bridewealth in Southern Africa. 224 pp.*
Lloyd, P. C. Power and Independence. *Urban Africans' Perception of Social Inequality. 264 pp.*
Malinowski, B. and **de la Fuente, J.** Malinowski in Mexico. *The Economics of a Mexican Market System. Edited and Introduced by Susan Drucker-Brown. About 240 pp.*
Parry, J. P. Caste and Kinship in Kangra. *352 pp. Illustrated.*
Pettigrew, Joyce. Robber Noblemen. *A Study of the Political System of the Sikh Jats. 284 pp.*
Street, Brian V. The Savage in Literature. *Representations of 'Primitive' Society in English Fiction, 1858–1920. 207 pp.*
Van Den Berghe, Pierre L. Power and Privilege at an African University. *278 pp.*

International Library of Phenomenology and Moral Sciences
General Editor   John O'Neill

Adorno, T. W. Aesthetic Theory. Translated by C. Lenhardt.
Apel, K.-O. Towards a Transformation of Philosophy. *308 pp.*
Bologh, R. W. Dialectical Phenomenology. *Marx's Method. 287 pp.*
Fekete, J. The Critical Twilight. *Explorations in the Ideology of Anglo-American Literary Theory from Eliot to McLuhan. 300 pp.*
Green, B. S. Knowing the Poor. *A Case Study in Textual Reality Construction. 200 pp.*
McHoul, A. W. How Texts Talk. *Essays on Reading and Ethnomethodology. 163 pp.*
Medina, A. Reflection, Time and the Novel. *Towards a Communicative Theory of Literature. 143 pp.*
O'Neill, J. Essaying Montaigne. *A Study of the Renaissance Institution of Writing and Reading. 244 pp.*
Schutz. A. Life Forms and Meaning Structure. *Translated, Introduced and Annotated by Helmut Wagner. 207 pp.*

International Library of Social Policy
General Editor   Kathleen Jones

Bayley, M. Mental Handicap and Community Care. *426 pp.*
Bottoms, A. E. and **McClean, J. D.** Defendants in the Criminal Process. *284 pp.*
Bradshaw, J. The Family Fund. *An Initiative in Social Policy. 248 pp.*
Butler, J. R. Family Doctors and Public Policy. *208 pp.*
Davies, Martin. Prisoners of Society. *Attitudes and Aftercare. 204 pp.*
Gittus, Elizabeth. Flats, Families and the Under-Fives. *285 pp.*
Holman, Robert. Trading in Children. *A Study of Private Fostering. 355 pp.*
Jeffs, A. Young People and the Youth Service. *160 pp.*
Jones, Howard and **Cornes, Paul.** Open Prisons. *288 pp.*
Jones, Kathleen. History of the Mental Health Service. *428 pp.*

Jones, Kathleen with **Brown, John, Cunningham, W. J., Roberts, Julian** and **Williams, Peter.** Opening the Door. *A Study of New Policies for the Mentally Handicapped. 278 pp.*

Karn, Valerie. Retiring to the Seaside. *400 pp. 2 maps. Numerous tables.*

King, R. D. and **Elliot, K. W.** Albany: Birth of a Prison—End of an Era. *294 pp.*

Thomas, J. E. The English Prison Officer since 1850. *258 pp.*

Walton, R. G. Women in Social Work. *303 pp.*

● **Woodward, J.** To Do the Sick No Harm. *A Study of the British Voluntary Hospital System to 1875. 234 pp.*

International Library of Welfare and Philosophy
General Editors Noel Timms and David Watson

○ **Campbell, J.** The Left and Rights. *A Conceptual Analysis of the Idea of Socialist Rights. About 296 pp.*

● **McDermott, F. E.** (Ed.) Self-Determination in Social Work. *A Collection of Essays on Self-determination and Related Concepts by Philosophers and Social Work Theorists.* Contributors: *F. P. Biestek, S. Bernstein, A. Keith-Lucas, D. Sayer, H. H. Perelman, C. Whittington, R. F. Stalley, F. E. McDermott, I. Berlin, H. J. McCloskey, H. L. A. Hart, J. Wilson, A. I. Melden, S. I. Benn. 254 pp.*

● **Plant, Raymond.** Community and Ideology. *104 pp.*

● **Plant, Raymond, Lesser, Harry** and **Taylor-Gooby, Peter.** Political Philosophy and Social Welfare. *Essays on the Normative Basis of Welfare Provision. 276 pp.*

Ragg, N. M. People Not Cases. *A Philosophical Approach to Social Work. 168 pp.*

Timms, Noel (Ed.) Social Welfare. *Why and How? 316 pp. 7 figures.*

● **Timms, Noel** and **Watson, David** (Eds) Talking About Welfare. *Readings in Philosophy and Social Policy.* Contributors: *T. H. Marshall, R. B. Brandt, G. H. von Wright, K. Nielsen, M. Cranston, R. M. Titmuss, R. S. Downie, E. Telfer, D. Donnison, J. Benson, P. Leonard. A. Keith-Lucas, D. Walsh, I. T. Ramsey. 230 pp.*

● Philosophy in Social Work. *250 pp.*

● **Weale, A.** Equality and Social Policy. *164 pp.*

Library of Social Work
General Editor Noel Timms

● **Baldock, Peter.** Community Work and Social Work. *140 pp.*

○ **Beedell, Christopher.** Residential Life with Children. *210 pp. Crown 8vo.*

● **Berry, Juliet.** Daily Experience in Residential Life. *A Study of Children and their Care-givers. 202 pp.*

○ Social Work with Children. *190 pp. Crown 8vo.*

● **Brearley, C. Paul.** Residential Work with the Elderly. *116 pp.*

● Social Work, Ageing and Society. *126 pp.*

● **Cheetham, Juliet.** Social Work with Immigrants. *240 pp. Crown 8vo.*

● **Cross, Crispin P.** (Ed.) Interviewing and Communication in Social Work. *Contributions by C. P. Cross, D. Laurenson, B. Strutt, S. Raven. 192 pp. Crown 8vo.*

● **Curnock, Kathleen** and **Hardiker, Pauline.** Towards Practice Theory. *Skills and Methods in Social Assessments. 208 pp.*

● **Davies, Bernard.** The Use of Groups in Social Work Practice. *158 pp.*

Davies, Bleddyn and **Knapp, M.** Old People's Homes and the Production of Welfare. *264 pp.*

12

● **Davies, Martin.** Support Systems in Social Work. *144 pp.*
Ellis, June. (Ed.) West African Families in Britain. *A Meeting of Two Cultures. Contributions by Pat Stapleton, Vivien Biggs. 150 pp. 1 map.*
○ **Ford, J.** Human Behaviour. *Towards a Practical Understanding. About 160 pp.*
● **Hart, John.** Social Work and Sexual Conduct. *230 pp.*
Heraud, Brian. Training for Uncertainty. *A Sociological Approach to Social Work Education. 138 pp.*
Holder, D. and **Wardle, M.** Teamwork and the Development of a Unitary Approach. *212 pp.*
● **Hutten, Joan M.** Short-Term Contracts in Social Work. *Contributions by Stella M. Hall, Elsie Osborne, Mannie Sher, Eva Sternberg, Elizabeth Tuters. 134 pp.*
Jackson, Michael P. and **Valencia, B. Michael.** Financial Aid Through Social Work. *140 pp.*
● **Jones, Howard.** The Residential Community. *A Setting for Social Work. 150 pp.*
● (Ed.) Towards a New Social Work. *Contributions by Howard Jones, D. A. Fowler, J. R. Cypher, R. G. Walton, Geoffrey Mungham, Philip Priestley, Ian Shaw, M. Bartley, R. Deacon, Irwin Epstein, Geoffrey Pearson. 184 pp.*
Jones, Ray and **Pritchard, Colin.** (Eds) Social Work With Adolescents. *Contributions by Ray Jones, Colin Pritchard, Jack Dunham, Florence Rossetti, Andrew Kerslake, John Burns, William Gregory, Graham Templeman, Kenneth E. Reid, Audrey Taylor.*
○ **Jordon, William.** The Social Worker in Family Situations. *160 pp. Crown 8vo.*
● **Laycock, A. L.** Adolescents and Social Work. *128 pp. Crown 8vo.*
● **Lees, Ray.** Politics and Social Work. *128 pp. Crown 8vo.*
● Research Strategies for Social Welfare. *112 pp. Tables.*
○ **McCullough, M. K.** and **Ely, Peter J.** Social Work with Groups. *127 pp. Crown 8vo.*
● **Moffett, Jonathan.** Concepts in Casework Treatment. *128 pp. Crown 8vo.*
Parsloe, Phyllida. Juvenile Justice in Britain and the United States. *The Balance of Needs and Rights. 336 pp.*
● **Plant, Raymond.** Social and Moral Theory in Casework. *112 pp. Crown 8vo.*
Priestley, Philip, Fears, Denise and **Fuller, Roger.** Justice for Juveniles. *The 1969 Children and Young Persons Act: A Case for Reform? 128 pp.*
● **Pritchard, Colin** and **Taylor, Richard.** Social Work: Reform or Revolution? *170 pp.*
○ **Pugh, Elisabeth.** Social Work in Child Care. *128 pp. Crown 8vo.*
● **Robinson, Margaret.** Schools and Social Work. *282 pp.*
○ **Ruddock, Ralph.** Roles and Relationships. *128 pp. Crown 8vo.*
● **Sainsbury, Eric.** Social Diagnosis in Casework. *118 pp. Crown 8vo.*
● **Sainsbury, Eric, Phillips, David** and **Nixon, Stephen.** Social Work in Focus. *Clients' and Social Workers' Perceptions in Long-Term Social Work. 220 pp.*
● Social Work with Families. *Perceptions of Social Casework among Clients of a Family Service. 188pp.*
Seed, Philip. The Expansion of Social Work in Britain. *128 pp. Crown 8vo.*
● **Shaw, John.** The Self in Social Work. *124 pp.*
Smale, Gerald G. Prophecy, Behaviour and Change. *An Examination of Self-fulfilling Prophecies in Helping Relationships. 116 pp. Crown 8vo.*
Smith, Gilbert. Social Need. *Policy, Practice and Research. 155 pp.*
● Social Work and the Sociology of Organisations. *124 pp. Revised edition.*
● **Sutton, Carole.** Psychology for Social Workers and Counsellors. *An Introduction. 248 pp.*
● **Timms, Noel.** Language of Social Casework. *122 pp. Crown 8vo.*

● Recording in Social Work. *124 pp. Crown 8vo.*
● **Todd, F. Joan.** Social Work with the Mentally Subnormal. *96 pp. Crown 8vo.*
● **Walrond-Skinner, Sue.** Family Therapy. *The Treatment of Natural Systems.*
    172 pp.
● **Warham, Joyce.** An Introduction to Administration for Social Workers.
    Revised edition. 112 pp.
● An Open Case. *The Organisational Context of Social Work. 172 pp.*
○ **Wittenberg, Isca Salzberger.** Psycho-Analytic Insight and Relationships.
    A Kleinian Approach. 196 pp. Crown 8vo.

Primary Socialization, Language and Education

General Editor   Basil Bernstein

Adlam, Diana S., *with the assistance of Geoffrey Turner and Lesley Lineker.*
    Code in Context. *272 pp.*
Bernstein, Basil. Class, Codes and Control. *3 volumes.*
●   1. *Theoretical Studies Towards a Sociology of Language. 254 pp.*
     2. *Applied Studies Towards a Sociology of Language. 377 pp.*
●   3. *Towards a Theory of Educational Transmission. 167 pp.*
Brandis, Walter and **Henderson, Dorothy.** Social Class, Language and
    Communication. *288 pp.*
Cook-Gumperz, Jenny. Social Control and Socialization. *A Study of Class
    Differences in the Language of Maternal Control. 290 pp.*
● **Gahagan, D. M.** and **G. A.** Talk Reform. *Exploration in Language for Infant
    School Children. 160 pp.*
Hawkins, P. R. Social Class, the Nominal Group and Verbal Strategies. *About
    220 pp.*
Robinson, W. P. and **Rakstraw, Susan D. A.** A Question of Answers.
    2 volumes. 192 pp. and 180 pp.
Turner, Geoffrey J. and **Mohan, Bernard A.** A Linguistic Description and
    Computer Programme for Children's Speech. *208 pp.*

Reports of the Institute of Community Studies

Baker, J. The Neighbourhood Advice Centre. A Community Project in
    Camden. *320 pp.*
● **Cartwright, Ann.** Patients and their Doctors. *A Study of General Practice.
    304 pp.*
Dench, Geoff. Maltese in London. *A Case-study in the Erosion of Ethnic
    Consciousness. 302 pp.*
Jackson, Brian and **Marsden, Dennis.** Education and the Working Class: *Some
    General Themes Raised by a Study of 88 Working-class Children in a
    Northern Industrial City. 268 pp. 2 folders.*
Madge, C. and **Willmott, P.** Inner City Poverty in Paris and London. *144 pp.*
Marris, Peter. The Experience of Higher Education. *232 pp. 27 tables.*
● Loss and Change. *192 pp.*
Marris, Peter and **Rein, Martin.** Dilemmas of Social Reform. *Poverty and
    Community Action in the United States. 256 pp.*
Marris, Peter and **Somerset, Anthony.** African Businessmen. *A Study of
    Entrepreneurship and Development in Kenya. 256 pp.*
Mills, Richard. Young Outsiders: *a Study in Alternative Communities. 216 pp.*
Runciman, W. G. Relative Deprivation and Social Justice. *A Study of Attitudes
    to Social Inequality in Twentieth-Century England. 352 pp.*

Willmott, Peter. Adolescent Boys in East London. *230 pp.*
Willmott, Peter and **Young, Michael.** Family and Class in a London Suburb. *202 pp. 47 tables.*
Young, Michael and **McGeeney, Patrick.** Learning Begins at Home. *A Study of a Junior School and its Parents. 128 pp.*
Young, Michael and **Willmott, Peter.** Family and Kinship in East London. *Foreword by Richard M. Titmuss. 252 pp. 39 tables.*
The Symmetrical Family. *410 pp.*

Reports of the Institute for Social Studies in Medical Care

Cartwright, Ann, Hockey, Lisbeth and **Anderson, John J.** Life Before Death. *310 pp.*
Dunnell, Karen and **Cartwright, Ann.** Medicine Takers, Prescribers and Hoarders. *190 pp.*
Farrell, C. My Mother Said. . . *A Study of the Way Young People Learned About Sex and Birth Control. 288 pp.*

Medicine, Illness and Society
General Editor W. M. Williams

Hall, David J. Social Relations & Innovation. *Changing the State of Play in Hospitals. 232 pp.*
Hall, David J. and **Stacey M.** (Eds) Beyond Separation. *234 pp.*
Robinson, David. The Process of Becoming Ill. *142 pp.*
Stacey, Margaret *et al.* Hospitals, Children and Their Families. *The Report of a Pilot Study. 202 pp.*
Stimson, G. V. and **Webb, B.** Going to See the Doctor. *The Consultation Process in General Practice. 155 pp.*

Monographs in Social Theory
General Editor Arthur Brittan

● **Barnes, B.** Scientific Knowledge and Sociological Theory. *192 pp.*
Bauman, Zygmunt. Culture as Praxis. *204 pp.*
● **Dixon, Keith.** Sociological Theory. *Pretence and Possibility. 142 pp.*
The Sociology of Belief. *Fallacy and Foundation. 144 pp.*
Goff, T. W. Marx and Mead. *Contributions to a Sociology of Knowledge. 176 pp.*
Meltzer, B. N., Petras, J. W. and **Reynolds, L. T.** Symbolic Interactionism. *Genesis, Varieties and Criticisms. 144 pp.*
● **Smith, Anthony D.** The Concept of Social Change. *A Critique of the Functionalist Theory of Social Change. 208 pp.*
● **Tudor, Andrew.** Beyond Empiricism. *Philosophy of Science in Sociology. 224 pp.*

Routledge Social Science Journals

The British Journal of Sociology. *Editor – Angus Stewart; Associate Editor – Leslie Sklair. Vol. 1, No. 1 – March 1950 and Quarterly. Roy. 8vo. All back issues available. An international journal publishing original papers in the field of sociology and related areas.*

Community Work. *Edited by David Jones and Majorie Mayo. 1973. Published annually.*

Economy and Society. *Vol. 1, No. 1. February 1972 and Quarterly. Metric Roy. 8vo. A journal for all social scientists covering sociology, philosophy, anthropology, economics and history. All back numbers available.*

Ethnic and Racial Studies. *Editor – John Stone. Vol. 1 – 1978. Published quarterly.*

Religion. Journal of Religion and Religions. *Chairman of Editorial Board, Ninian Smart. Vol. 1, No. 1, Spring 1971. A journal with an inter-disciplinary approach to the study of the phenomena of religion. All back numbers available.*

Sociological Review. *Chairman of Editorial Board, S. J. Eggleston. New Series. August 1982, Vol. 30, No. 1. Published quarterly.*

Sociology of Health and Illness. *A Journal of Medical Sociology. Editor – Alan Davies; Associate Editor – Ray Jobling. Vol. 1, Spring 1979. Published 3 times per annum.*

Year Book of Social Policy in Britain. *Edited by Kathleen Jones. 1971. Published annually.*

Social and Psychological Aspects of Medical Practice
Editor Trevor Silverstone

Lader, Malcolm. Psychophysiology of Mental Illness. *280 pp.*

● **Silverstone, Trevor** and **Turner, Paul.** Drug Treatment in Psychiatry. *Third edition. 256 pp.*

Whiteley, J. S. and **Gordon, J.** Group Approaches in Psychiatry. *240 pp.*